Exploring tough questions facing youth today

GOD IS A WARRIOR?
Violence in the Bible

ISBN 978-1-949628-11-1
Printed in the United States of America.
10 9 8 7 6 5 4 3 2 1   22 21 20 19

Published by The Pastoral Center, http://pastoral.center.

Developed in partnership with MennoMedia and Brethren Press. Series editors: Fumiaki Tosu, Ann Naffziger, and Paul Canavese. *God Is a Warrior?* Writer, David Radcliff. Project editor, Lani Wright. Staff editors, Susan E. Janzen, Julie Garber, and James Deaton. Updated design, Paul Stocksdale.

All rights reserved. Purchase of this book includes a license to reproduce this resource for use in a single parish, school, or other similar organization. You are allowed to share and make unlimited copies only for use within the organization that licensed it. If you serve more than one organization, each should purchase its own license. You may not post this document to any web site without explicit permission to do so. Outside of these conditions, no part of this book may be reproduced in any form or by any means, electronic or mechanical, including photocopying, recording, taping, or via any retrieval system, without the written permission of The Pastoral Center, 1212 Versailles Ave., Alameda, CA 94501. Thank you for cooperating with our honor system regarding our licenses.

For questions or to order additional copies or licenses, please call 1-844-727-8672 or visit http://pastoral.center.

Portions of this work © 2019 by The Pastoral Center / PastoralCenter.com. Adapted and published with permission from Generation Why Bible Studies. © 1997, 2015 Brethren Press, Elgin, IL 60120 and MennoMedia, Harrisonburg, VA 22803, U.S.A. All rights reserved.

Unless otherwise noted, the Scripture passages contained herein are from the *New Revised Standard Version of the Bible*, copyright © 1989 by the National Council of the Churches of Christ in the United States of America. Used by permission. All rights reserved.

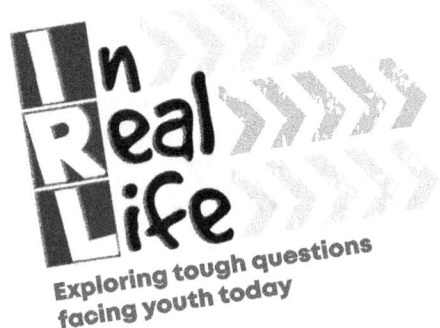

Bible-based Explorations of Issues Facing Youth

>> OVERVIEW

When conversing online, the acronym IRL stands for "in real life." The virtual world of social media, text chats, blogs, and more have the power to remove us from the real world. What we experience online can skew our perspective on what it means to be human. It can numb us, incite us, distract us, depress us, confuse us, and make us rude or impatient. Strangely, this supposedly "social" and "connected" technology can profoundly disconnect us from others.

Religious faith can also place us in a bubble, especially when it distances us from others. When we keep the prophetic message at a safe distance, obscured in theological language and abstractions, we are missing the whole point. And when we see our parish as an insider club that serves itself, we can forget the radically inclusive message entrusted to us: God's love is for *everyone*, and God expects us to transform the *whole world* through that love.

Through the incarnation, God showed up in the real world to show us that our faith is not just about talking the talk, but also walking the walk. It can be risky. It can be confusing. It can hurt. But living out our faith can also bring us great purpose, peace, and joy.

This series connects the Bible with the tough questions that youth (and adults) encounter in their neighborhood, in school, among friends, and even online. This process will help you as a leader break open these issues in a fun and meaningful way, sparking conversation and the kind of life change Jesus invites us to embrace.

>> THE ROLE OF PARENTS

As children enter middle school and high school, they become more independent, self-reliant, and, well, self-centered. This can bring parents to make assumptions that this is the time to step back, giving their child more space to form their identity. While there is truth to that at some level (adolescents definitely shouldn't be smothered), this is a stage of life when parents should in fact *lean in*. The apparent confidence and bluster youth show on the outside can mask the insecurity and confusion on the inside. Youth need their parents to be involved more than ever.

>> WHOLE FAMILY FORMATION

Parents are the primary teachers of their own children, and parishes are waking up to the fact that faith formation programs need to bring parents into the process if they hope to see faith passed on to the next generation. Recent studies give us more and more evidence that the role of parents is the most important factor in determining whether a child will embrace faith as they move toward adulthood. Research from the Center for the Applied Research on the Apostolate shows that parents who talk about their faith and show through their actions that their faith is important to them are more likely to have children who remain Catholic.

More about Whole Family Formation

To learn more about how your parish can take a comprehensive whole family approach to faith formation, visit **GrowingUpCatholic.com**.

While whole family events with elementary-aged children are on the rise, the role of parents can be an afterthought in youth ministry. We have designed the sessions in this series to work with or without parents present, and we encourage you to offer them as parent-child events.

If you choose to involve parents, it is important to consider before each session how to best do so. Many of the activities in this series are high-energy, creative, or silly. Some parents may need some encouragement to get out of their heads and have fun with the group. A few activities involving physical contact would be inappropriate for parents and youth to participate together, and we have noted them as such.

There are a number of ways to approach discussions with parent participation. Unless you have a small group, you will likely want to break into smaller groups for conversation. Some youth may be self-conscious and unable to be completely honest and open in a group situation with a parent present. For this reason, you may choose in some cases to assign parents to different groups from their own children, or to have separate parent and child groups altogether. Be sure to cover expectations around confidentiality. It is inappropriate for a parent (or youth) to share with another parent what their child said in a small group.

Note that even if parents and their children do not share all conversations together in the session, they will still have a valuable shared experience and can have extended conversations about it later.

THANK YOU

The role you play in gathering, animating, praying with, and forming youth is a valuable one. Thank you for all you do to serve the church and its families!

Bible-based Explorations of Issues Facing Youth

GOD IS A WARRIOR?
Violence in the Bible

>> INTRODUCTION

Is the Bible friend or foe to the peacemaker? How do we cope with the seeming contrasting pictures of a sectarian warrior God and a God of suffering, self-sacrificing love? The Bible challenges us to be reconciled to one another and to work for justice. Then what do we do with stories that either seem to condone violence or even to encourage it?

It's not hard to find graphic violence in the scriptures, along with a God who seems to sanction it. The stories of Israel's conquest of Canaan have such troubling elements; but the book of Judges is a reminder that this "conquest" was not as complete or as easily achieved as the writer of Joshua would have us believe.

Yet it is also in the Hebrew Bible that we find violence and injustice confronted and condemned as early as the stories of creation and as late as the ringing words of the prophet that nations will someday beat their swords into plowshares and study war no more.

When we encounter Jesus, we discover a God who has (mostly) retired the boxing gloves, and instead issued a call to nonviolence and unlimited love, except in some passages warning about the consequences in the after life for those who don't do God's will. While God incarnate in Jesus gives us the clearest image of God's love and character, we are still plagued with how to follow a Jesus storming through the Temple, or what to think about Jesus' disciples ready to call down fire on a whole village. What do we do when violence seems justified? When it has a noble motive? How will we live with hope when a violent world seems to be burning down around us?

Dedicated, Bible-reading Christians have come out boldly on both sides of the violence/nonviolence issue. Some point to stories of war in the Hebrew Bible as justification for their participation in war. Others cite Jesus' words and example to lay a case *against* war.

Youth, who are quick to detect inconsistency in what they hear, jump on this biblical dilemma. This unit digs deeper, however, to tell the "rest of the story," leading you and your youth to grapple with these tough questions with the help of new insight and information about the Bible stories of "violence." Perhaps you all will come to a new commitment to God's way of healing and reconciling.

Preparation Alert >>>>

A number of sessions ask for you to get information concerning contemporary situations in which violence is occurring. Some contacts are in the resources section below. You may want to browse through that list and supplement your resources (through Internet searches, libraries, etc.) before you start the unit.

EXTENDER SESSION

Extender sessions suggest special activities related to the issue of the unit. They help accommodate the diversity of parish schedules. Since each unit is undated, participants may study units in their entirety and still participate in special events of the parish that get scheduled simultaneously with youth group time. Extender sessions can be used anytime, but the one for this unit best follows **Session 5**. Calculate now whether or not you will be using the extender session.

THE TEACHING PLAN: The parts of the session guide

- **Faith story.** The session is rooted in this Bible passage.
- **Faith focus.** The story of the passage in a nutshell.
- **Session goal.** The entire session is built around this goal. What changes—in knowledge, attitude, and/or action—do you desire in your group?
- **Materials needed and advance preparation.** This is what you will need if the session is to go smoothly. You'll feel more at ease if you've taken care of these details before you meet your group.

FROM LIFE TO BIBLE TO LIFE

The teaching plan is called *life-centered*. However, when we write each session, we always begin with scripture. We ask, what does this particular passage say, especially to youth? Each session moves from life to Bible to life. So the Bible is really at the center of this way of teaching.

In every session we try to hit upon a tough question that participants might ask. Find out what questions on this issue are important for your group. Feel free to bring your own input and invite your group members to add their own experiences.

TEACHING THE SESSION

The five step-by-step movements will carry you from *life to the Bible and back to life*. Each session takes about 45 to 50 minutes. If there is a handout sheet for the session, take note of any complementary activities and stories.

1. **Focus.** Intended to create a friendly climate within the group and to *draw attention* to the issue.

2. **Connect.** Invites participants to *express* their own life experience about the issue, through talking, drawing, role playing, and other activities. Also uses memory, reason, or imagination to get the group thinking about *why* they view the issue the way they do.

3. **Explore the Bible.** What does the Bible *say* about the issue? With a minimum of lecturing, dig into the faith story and search for answers to questions raised in the first activities. The Insights from Scripture section will help clarify the faith story. Help participants discover how the faith community understands the Bible passage.

4. **Apply** the faith story. What does the Bible passage *mean* for contemporary life? This is the "aha!" moment when participants realize the faith story has wisdom for *their* lives.

5. **Respond.** Why does the Bible passage *matter*? What will the group do about the issue in light of what they have learned from their own experiences set alongside the faith story? How can we *live* the faith story rather than pass it off as a mere intellectual exercise?

LOOK AHEAD

Here are reminders for what you need to do for the next session or two.

INSIGHTS FROM SCRIPTURE

Here is a resource for Explore the Bible. Don't try to use all the material given. Take what you need to lead the session and answer questions your group may have. Let the Insights section inspire you to think and study more about the passage for the session.

>> HANDOUT SHEETS

Occasionally, there will be a handout sheet to complement your session. If you choose to use this, make enough copies for the group in advance of the session. These sheets may include questions, stories, agree/disagree exercises, charts, pictures, and other materials to stimulate thinking and discussion.

Generally, no participant preparation is required unless the session plan calls for you to contact selected group members for specific tasks.

FURTHER RESOURCES

Some of the activities in this unit were adapted from Eddy Hall's *Decide for Peace*, a study on conscientious objection to war.

>> BOOKS AND ARTICLES

Find a number of great options offered for sale by The Pastoral Center at https://pastoral.center/nonviolence, including *What Pope Francis Says about Peace*, *Threshold Bible Study: Peacemaking and Nonviolence*, *The Beatitudes of Peace*, *Fatima at 100*, *Fatima Today: 10 Steps to World Peace*, many of the resources listed below, and more.

Catholic Nonviolence Initiative maintains a list of resources on peace and nonviolence at https://nonviolencejustpeace.net/resources/.

The New Community Project maintains a reading list (http://www.newcommunityproject.org/reading-list.shtml) on earth care, global justice, and the process of change.

Butigan, Ken. *Nonviolent Lives*, explores the lives of dozens of modern-day nonviolent activists, from Cesar Chavez and Dorothy Day to present-day leaders like John Dear, Anne Symens-Bucher, and Medea Benjamin.

Douglass, Jim. *The Nonviolent Coming of God*, is an exploration of what it means to be a follower of Jesus in the nuclear age. The choice, he says, is between nonviolence and nonexistence.

Merton, Thomas. *Cold War Letters*, is a collection of personal letters written by the Catholic monk and peace activist to friends in 1961 and 1962, when censure by his superiors prevented him from publishing his ideas on nonviolence and peace any other way.

Merton, Thomas. *Passion for Peace*, is a collection of essays on the topic of peace and nonviolence.

Slattery, Laura, Veronica Pelicaric, and Ken Preston-Pile. *Engage: Exploring Nonviolent Living*, is a study program from Pace e Bene for learning, practicing, and experimenting with the power of creative nonviolence to transform our lives and our world.

The Power of Nonviolence, is an anthology of writings by peace advocates put together by Beacon Press. Contributors include Dorothy Day, Thomas Merton, Daniel Berrigan, and Martin Luther King, Jr.

Chenoweth, Erica and Maria Stephan, *Why Civil Resistance Works*, is a landmark scholarly work arguing that nonviolent movements for social change are twice as effective as violent movements in achieving their goals.

Easwaran, Eknath, *Gandhi the Man*, is an excellent biography of the man most responsible for introducing the world to nonviolence.

Grossman, Dave. *On Killing: The Psychological Cost of Learning to Kill in War and Society*. Former Army psychologist documents a powerful disinclination against the taking of human life, even among soldiers.

Hartsough, David, *Waging Peace: Global Adventures of a Lifelong Activist*.

Sider, Ronald. *Non-violence, The Invincible Weapon?* A book full of stories of how nonviolent methods were successfully used to fight violence. It sounds a call for Christians to risk their lives, just as armed soldiers do, to serve in a nonviolent peace army.

Ways Out: The Book of Changes for Peace. Ed. Gene Knudsen-Hoffman. John Daniel & Co. Ninety-eight ideas for making peace.

≫ AUDIOVISUAL RESOURCES

A Force More Powerful is an excellent video series, and would be a perfect compliment to this unit. The episodes are about 30 minutes each, and cover various nonviolent movements of the 20th century.

Anybody's Son Will Do, (https://youtu.be/DShDaJXK5qo) from Film Board of Canada, is available in six segments on YouTube. They take the viewer straight to Paris Island for a firsthand, upclose look at Marine Corps boot camp. Excellent counter-recruitment piece. 60 minutes.

≫ ORGANIZATIONS

Pax Christi USA (PaxChristiUSA.org), 415 Michigan Ave. NE Suite 240, Washington, DC 20017 (202-635-2741).

Catholic Nonviolence Initiative (NonviolenceJustPeace.net), a project of Pax Christi International, Rue du Progrès, 323, B-1030 Brussels, Belgium (+32(0)2-502-55-50).

Pace e Bene (PaceeBene.org), info@paceebene.org, (510-268-8765).

Catholic Peace Fellowship (CatholicPeaceFellowship.org), P.O. Box 4232, South Bend, IN 46634 (574-339-1100; e-mail: fornatl@igc.apc.org).

Fellowship of Reconciliation (FOR) (forusa.org/), P.O. Box 271, Nyack NY 10960 (914-358-4601; e-mail: fornatl@igc.apc.org).

On Earth Peace (OnEarthPeace.org), P.O. Box 188, 500 Main St., New Windsor MD 21776 (410-635-8704).

Amnesty International (amnesty.org)

Christian Peacemaker Teams (cpt.org), PO Box 6508, Chicago IL 60680 (312-455-1199, e-mail: cpt@igc.apc.org).

Heifer International (heifer.org), 1 World Avenue, Little Rock AR 72202 (855.9HUNGER, 855.948.6437).

Exploring tough questions facing youth today

>>> SESSION 1

ALL THE KING'S HORSES >>>

>> KEY VERSE

And the Lord said to Joshua, "Do not be afraid of them, for tomorrow at this time I will hand over all of them, slain, to Israel; you shall hamstring their horses, and burn their chariots with fire." (Joshua 11:6)

>> FAITH STORY

Joshua 11

>> FAITH FOCUS

Following their exodus from Egypt, the Israelite people entered the land of Canaan, the land promised to them by God (Deuteronomy 6:22-23). But this area already had a name and it was already inhabited—by the Canaanites. If the Israelites wanted the land for their own, they would have to expel the original inhabitants by force. The kings of Canaan massed together against the invaders (Israel), but were soundly defeated by a military captain who ruthlessly followed the battle instructions of his God. How do we today understand God's seeming approval of violence as the primary means for the Israelites to take over the land of Canaan?

>> SESSION GOAL

Lead participants to begin to reconcile two contrasting images of God: a "warrior" God and the God of love embodied in Jesus.

TEACHING PLAN

1. FOCUS 10 minutes

>> **Option A:** Perform the skit "A Moving Experience" (first handout sheet).

Enlist the help of the junior high or other small groups to play the role of the conquerors in a skit. If this is not possible, the youngest members of the youth group could play this role. Provide the junior high leader with a script at least one week in advance, and encourage them to use props to enhance their role of "conquerors" (marching in, waving banners, etc.).

>> Materials needed and advance preparation

- Contact junior high leader to combine groups for part of this session (see Focus)

- Copies of the handout sheets for Session 1 (*Option A* in Focus and *Option B* in Apply)

- Role of wide masking or duct tape to mark a playing area (*Option B* in Focus)

- Chalkboard/chalk or newsprint/marker

- Pile of fist-sized rocks or bricks, about one per person (*Option A* in Apply)

- Descriptions of "Warrior God" and "Prince of Peace" (*Option B* in Apply')

- Bibles

- Bible concordances

- Writing paper and pencils/pens (*Option B* in Respond)

As you open the session, give the participants copies of the skit, dividing the "current resident" parts among the group. (**Note:** If there are more than four participants who want to have a speaking part, divide parts accordingly, or double up if you have just one or two people.) Have them read the preface and briefly look over their parts prior to the arrival of the "conquerors." Let the invasion begin!

Continue with **Option A** under Connect, below.

>> **Option B** Play "Bump Out." Mark a square playing area 10-15 feet across, smaller or larger depending on the size of your group. Divide into teams of four people each. Each team huddles together with arms locked inside the playing area. The goal is to bump all the other teams from the playing area. Last team inside the playing area is the winner.

Rules:
- Use only hips to bump out other teams.
- Arms must remain locked.
- Team is not out of the game until every member is outside the playing area. When that happens, the team sits and waits for game to finish.

(game adapted from *Screamers and Scramblers*, by Michael W. Capps)

Declare a winner, call them the "Israelites," and continue with the short interview under Connect, **Option B**, below.

> "To be true followers of Jesus today also includes embracing his teaching about nonviolence."
>
> Pope Francis
> Message for World Day of Peace 2017

2. CONNECT 5-7 minutes

>> **Option A:** (At this point, junior high kids may either stay or leave. If they leave, omit questions pertaining to the "conquerors.")

Process the skit by asking how both youth and junior high kids felt about their respective roles.

- *How did you "current residents" feel about another group coming in and telling you they were taking over the room?*
- *You "conquerors," did you feel a sense of power knowing that God had told you that the room was yours and that you would be able to easily drive out the people who were already there?*
- *How "fair" is it for one group to try to do it to another group?*
- *Do you know of places in the world where this has actually happened in history, or is happening now?* (Examples include: Tibet's occupation by China; Indonesia taking over East Timor; Europeans "conquering" the Americas.)

>> **Option B:** Interview the "conquering Israelites," asking, *Did you have any special technique for bumping that helped you win?* (Wait for response.) Then ask, *What if I, the leader, had told you at the beginning of the game that I really wanted you to win, that I was rooting for you, and would see that you win? Would that have made any difference to you? To the other teams?*

3. EXPLORE THE BIBLE 10 minutes

Shift to this activity by saying: *Invasion happens. But what makes it really potent is when one party believes that God is fighting along with them and for them. We have pictures of this "warrior" God in the Bible. Let's see what one looks like....*

Read the story of violence aloud from Joshua 11:1-9. Then ask:

- *What do you think the biblical writer is trying to convey here?*
- *Is this merely an example of the human tendency to glorify the past, making complex situations seem much more clear cut? Or is there something about how God is portrayed here that is at the core of who God is and what God is about in the world?*

Solicit some responses, then offer these helps:

We can take comfort that Jesus himself had to wrestle with some of these questions. Jesus stated more than once, "You have heard it said..., but I say to you...". Without throwing out God's revelation of the past, Jesus put God in a new light. It might be said that in Jesus we finally got a crystal clear look at God, rather than the portrait-shrouded-in-mist we had to go on in the past.

Ask the group how they fit this picture of God—where God is actively involved in the destruction of another group—with the God they know through Jesus—where we learn that we are to love our enemies. Take a poll to discover the way various group members deal with these different understandings of God. Give as options the following:

- The understanding of God changed over the years, with people of an earlier time understanding God differently than people did at the time of Jesus.
- God changed over the years, realizing that violence was not the best way to achieve change in human life;
- The people who wrote this part of the Bible gave in to the human tendency to glorify their past, wanting to make it clear that God was with them every step of the way and justifying their entry into the promised land;
- These are just two sides of the same God—even today, God condones violence towards others as an acceptable way of dealing with other people or nations.

After reading the various options (and adding other choices), have the group rank the choices, giving the highest number to their favorite option. For instance, if there are four options, each person's top choice would receive a "four" and their lowest choice a "one." Add up the totals for each option, and divide by the total number of people in the group.

4. APPLY 10-15 minutes

 Option A: Help the group explore how people today continue to think about God in the way that Joshua and the Israelites did. As each statement below is read, ask people to decide whether or not they agree with it. If they agree, they should stand and **pick a rock or brick** out of the pile (Stone Age weapons, remember?), and remain standing until the next question. If they *disagree* they should stay seated. Discuss each statement after the participants have indicated their agreement/disagreement with it.

1. God takes sides during a battle or war.
2. Many people in our country think that God is on our side, especially during a time of war.
3. If God were on anybody's side today, it would be on the side of the weak and poor, regardless of whether or not they believed in God.
4. People who fight a war thinking that God is on their side are likely to be more aggressive and fight with more vengeance than those who don't feel this way.

Continue with **Option A** under Respond, below.

>>>
"The whole world must summon the courage and technical means to say 'no' to nuclear conflict; 'no' to weapons of mass destruction; 'no' to an arms race that robs the poor and vulnerable… Peacemaking is not an optional commitment. It is a requirement of our faith. We are called to be peacemakers, not by some movement of the moment, but by our Lord Jesus."

The U.S. Bishops,
The Challenge of Peace: God's Promise and Our Response, 333.

>> **Option B: Hebrew Bible vs. New Testament**

Before the session, make one copy each of the two descriptions on the second handout sheet. If your group is larger than 16, make two copies of each description.

Form two groups (four groups if you have more than 16 people). Give the "Warrior God" description to half the groups and the "Prince of Peace" description to the other half. Give the following instructions: *Have you ever felt that the Hebrew Bible and New Testament send out different messages about war and peace? Group one's assignment is to make the case, using the Hebrew Bible, that it is God's will for people of faith to fight in war. Group two's assignment is to make the case, using the New Testament, that Jesus calls us to nonviolence.*

Say something like: *In this activity, you won't necessarily be expressing your own views. Your assignment is to make the strongest case you can for the position assigned to you.*

Distribute Bibles and concordances. Give the groups about 10 minutes to prepare their presentations. Each group should select one or two people to present the case developed by the group.

Have the Hebrew Bible group present first, then the New Testament group.

Ask, *How do you explain the difference between what the Hebrew Bible says about war and the New Testament teachings that seem to point to a much different way of relating to enemies?*

The key insight: Though we may not be able to explain exactly why God raised the ethical standard for relating to enemies, Jesus clearly calls his followers to a different standard than that of the ancient Hebrew law. We do not have to be able to answer all the whys to know what Jesus calls us to do.

Continue with **Option B** under Respond, below.

(activity adapted from Eddy Hall's *Decide for Peace*)

>>> **LOOK AHEAD**

Next time we'll look at the biblical notion of holy war, and God's strange set of rules for fighting.

5. RESPOND 5-10 minutes

Remind participants that one part of God's command to Joshua was that after the battle was over, the Israelites were to burn the chariots and disable the horses of the enemy. Why? Perhaps God wanted to keep the Israelites from learning to use the same weapons as their enemies. God wants victory to come because of the people's faith, not because of their superior weapons. (Choose one of the options below.)

>> **Option A:** Now use the rocks that symbolized weapons of destruction in "Apply" (above) to build something *constructive*. Choose a corner of your meeting space to build a monument to God—an altar. Joshua, too, built altars to God (Joshua 8:30), because he understood where his real power lay. Simply dry stack the rocks into a cone or square shape, then gather for a closing prayer around it. Ask God to teach us to trust our rock of salvation, and to help us transform weapons of destruction into monuments to peace. If possible, leave the altar standing as a reminder of this session.

>> **Option B:** The governments of the world spend a tremendous amount of money on weapons. When nations consider reducing their federal budgets, cuts in "defense spending" are rarely considered. In what ways do such high levels of military spending actually lead to greater insecurity? How might our world be more secure if we instead focused on meeting people's needs?

Do some Internet research. Include Catholic and other faith-based organizations listed on p. 3 to find out which military weapons systems might be being considered for cancellation—or even being banned. Check out progress on a worldwide movement to ban the production of landmines, as these weapons live on long after the time of conflict is past, continuing to kill and maim civilians. (http://www.icbl.org/media/342067/icb009_chronology_a5_v4-pages.pdf) There is also debate about the use of drones (http://www.rollingstone.com/politics/news/the-rise-of-the-killer-drones-how-america-goes-to-war-in-secret-20120416) and their effect on civilian noncombatants (http://www.pri.org/stories/2013-10-22/us-drone-strikes-are-controversial-are-they-war-crimes).

Write individual letters (or jointly sign a petition) to government officials calling for reductions in military spending and/or a halt to the production of certain weapons that are especially inhumane.

INSIGHTS FROM SCRIPTURE

When the people of Israel recalled this story of victory, they saw the Lord at the heart of the conquest. It was God who called Israel into the land of promise. It was God who routed their adversaries. It was God who approved of and even commanded the wholesale eradication of the enemy.

What do we make of this? Is this simply a different understanding of God? Is this one and the same God we know in Jesus of Nazareth? These are some of the questions raised by this account of victorious battle and others like it.

These questions are at the heart of questions of hermeneutics—the way we interpret the Bible. How do we deal with troublesome passages such as this one? Even those who do not find this passage troublesome must still deal with Jesus' teachings about enemies and violence, which seem to stand in direct opposition to a passage such as this one.

We aren't sure *how* the God we see revealed in the love of Jesus could be a God who would order the obliteration of whole peoples, including their animals and their property. But in asking this question, we must consider the likely motive for writing the story. The book of Joshua relates stirring battles and victories—victories in which God was seen to be active. That was a far cry from the prevailing religions, in which gods of stone needed daily placating. This God was *different*. This God *cared* about a band of former slaves. What better way to prove God's care than by delivering to Israel what slaves crave—power over their own destinies, their own land? These are epics, stories embellished by accounts of heroism, which also proclaim under no uncertain terms that Yahweh was the true living God.

War doesn't decide who's right. War decides who's left.

» SUCCESS IN WAR?

In many ways, the story of Joshua's victory—no, *God's* victory—has its parallel in the words of blessing spoken of any modern nation's troops as they march off to war. When a president or prime minister or priest asks for God's protection and for the "success" of a war effort, are they not also asking for the destruction of the enemy—and for God to play a role in this destruction? In the late 1800s, American writer Mark Twain wrote a stunning piece called *The War Prayer*, in which a man stumbles into a church on Sunday morning and challenges the congregation to pray the "other side" of their prayers for military victory: for the destruction of people's homes, for the orphaning of little children, for the bloodying of teenage boys. Praying for one side to win means praying for the other side to be wiped out.

It is a documented fact that wars are more brutal when the participants are motivated by religious convictions. This is as true on an interpersonal level as on the international level. A religious zealot brings a certain passion and disdain for the opinions—or lives—of others. Thus, passages such as this one in Joshua tend to mirror the way that human beings—especially religious ones—deal with their adversaries, and the role that they assign God in these conflicts.

Israel's God was a new revelation, and required a different standard in obedience and commitment: a two-way covenant. Such explanations do not wipe out our questions. But as Christian author Eddy Hall writes, "We don't have to understand God fully to know that Jesus calls us to a higher standard, a standard of loving our enemies and returning good for evil."

Exploring tough questions facing youth today

SETTING:

The year 1200 B.C.E. The people of the Middle East are just entering the Iron Age (some are entering it faster than others). It is a time of great social and political change in the region.

PLAYERS:

The **Israelites** (the "conquerors"): You were led by God out of Egypt 40 years ago and are finally getting what was promised—the land of Canaan (the youth room). In order to get what's coming to you after all these years of wandering, you have been ordered by God to drive out all those who currently inhabit Canaan (the youth).

The **Canaanites** ("current residents") have been living in this land (youth room) for some time. You are understandably perplexed and angered by the arrival of this new group who claims your room for their own. To make matters worse, these invaders say they are backed up by a God you never heard of.

THE CONFRONTATION BEGINS:

Conqueror 1: O.K. you bunch of heathens, your time in this room is up! Be prepared to pack up and move out!

Conqueror 2: Yeah, because God has given us this room for our very own, and God has told us to drive out anyone who gets in our way.

Conqueror 3: In fact, God will be the one to personally see to your swift and violent end, should you resist.

Conqueror 4: Praise be to God, the great Liberator! (*shouts of praise from the conquerors*)

Current Resident (C.R.) 1: Could we hold on just a second here? There's obviously a misunderstanding.

C.R. 2: Yeah, we've been here for quite a while and this room is home to us.

C.R. 3: And one might conclude that since we were here first, this room really belongs to us.

Conqueror 2: You're the ones who don't really understand the situation. Our God, the One True God, the God who liberated us from the junior high room [or other space], is now giving us the senior high room.

C.R. 3: Well, suppose we don't know this God and don't really believe what you're saying?

Conqueror 4: Makes no difference. You guys are history in a few minutes.

C.R. 1: Oh yeah? Suppose we tell you that you don't seem to have much in a way of modern weapons, and that we have a whole bunch of state-of-the-art horses and chariots.

C.R. 2: Yeah, like didn't you people notice that the rest of the world had moved right on into the Iron Age? Look at you—no chariots, no iron spears—you're from the Stone Age!

Conqueror 1: No problemo. We just happen to have the most powerful weapon of all—the Lord God Almighty. We may not even have to lift a finger to handle your measly chariots.

Conqueror 3: Enough of these pleasantries. You people need to clear out—or else!

C.R. 4: Maybe we'll just take our chances with "or else"!

Conqueror 2: You'll be sorry!

Permission is granted to photocopy this handout for use with this session.

Hebrew Bible vs. New Covenant

Exploring tough questions facing youth today

WARRIOR GOD

"The Lord is a warrior" (Exodus 15:3). Debating position: God uses war to judge and direct nations. The Hebrew Bible shows that God sometimes tells people to take part in carrying out these purposes by fighting in war. Because we respect God, it is our duty to support war, which for some of us will involve fighting in war, when the war is for a just cause.

Related scriptures: Deuteronomy 2:14-15; 7:16; 20:10-20; Joshua 6:1-21; Judges 7:1-25.

PRINCE OF PEACE

"He is named...Prince of Peace" (Isaiah 9:6). Debating position: Jesus calls us to love our enemies, to overcome evil with good. He shows us how to do this, not only by his daily life, but by laying down his life for us, even when we behaved as his enemies. To follow Jesus is to fight evil as Jesus did, and not with violence.

Related scriptures: Matthew 5:38-39, 43-45; Luke 6:27-36; Matthew 26:52; Romans 5:8, 10; Romans 12:14, 17-21.

God Is a Warrior? : Session 1

OK to photocopy. Permission is granted to photocopy this handout for use with this session.

>>> **SESSION 2**

MILITARY BUILD-DOWN >>>

>> KEY VERSE

The Lord said to Gideon, "The troops with you are too many for me to give the Midianites into their hand. Israel would only take the credit away from me, saying, 'My own hand has delivered me.'" (Judges 7:2)

>> FAITH STORY

Judges 6 and 7

>> FAITH FOCUS

With God's assistance, the Israelites had entered the land of Canaan. The book of Judges is a reminder that the "conquest" of Canaan was not as complete or as easily achieved as the book of Joshua portrays it. In Judges, the people relied on a series of charismatic leaders to provide leadership in crisis situations. These charismatic leaders were specially chosen by God, as opposed to a king who rules because he is from a royal family. The story of Gideon is an example of the whole book's theme that obedience to and trust in God is the only guarantee of success for God's people.

>> SESSION GOAL

Help participants understand the function of holy wars in the ancient scriptures—to build and/or test trust in God.

>> Materials needed and advance preparation

- Low table, chair, or stool, and a blindfold (*Option A* in Focus)
- Make-up kits or hairstyling accessories (*Option C* in Focus)
- Copies of the handout sheets for Session 2.
- Bibles
- Contact someone to tell about a time when they had to put their trust in God (*Option A* in Apply).
- Chalkboard/chalk or newsprint/marker
- Pieces of torn-up towel or fabric (1 per person) and pins (straight or safety) (*Option* in Respond)
- Writing paper/pencils

TEACHING PLAN

1. FOCUS 10 minutes

>> **Option A:** (for groups who are new to trust falls): Ask for a volunteer (or recruit someone prior to the meeting). Have the volunteer stand on the edge of a low table, chair, or stool, facing away from the others. The other members are in two lines behind the person, facing each other, with each one grasping the arms of the person directly across from them at approximately waist height. They should be immediately behind the person on the low platform, thus forming a "landing pad" for the one falling. Have the person close their eyes or put on a blindfold, and, keeping the body straight, fall back into the arms of the other participants. After several people have taken the fall, ask: *Was it easy or hard to fall backwards? Why? Did the falling ones have a moment of doubt? What was it like to be a catcher?*

>> **Option B:** **(for groups of fewer than 6):** Experience a trust circle. Form a small circle about a forearm's length apart, with one person in the middle. The person in the middle closes their eyes or is blindfolded, with arms folded across the chest, hugging themselves. The others raise their hands to the height of the person in the middle. Keeping the body straight and feet planted, this person then leans toward the others' hands. They, in turn, gently push the person around the circle or back and forth across the circle. The key is for the one in the middle to allow the others to control the movement.

>> **Option C:** **(for groups who are very familiar with trust falls or circles):** Experience a "trust make-up application" or "trust hair styling." Pair up, then provide partners with make-up (lipstick, eye shadow, etc.), **OR** brush, comb, mousse, barrettes, scrunchies, etc to do the other person's face and/or hair. Have fun! Take photos if you dare!

2. CONNECT 5 minutes

Wind up the "trust" experience by asking: In what ways is trusting God like trusting someone to (choose appropriate one):

- catch you when you fall?
- change your appearance?

Do other people play a role in helping us learn about trust in God, or is it something we have to learn for ourselves? When are the times we are forced to trust God the most? Is it when we feel in control of ourselves and our situation, or when things are out of our control?

3. EXPLORE THE BIBLE 10 minutes

Shift to this activity by saying: *Trusting sometimes comes hard, especially if someone's asking you to give up control of something. A leader of the Israelites, Gideon, had plenty to learn about trusting God....*

To reconstruct the story, do the multiple choice "quiz" on the first handout sheet. Read the questions and have participants vote on the correct answer. After each one, mark the correct phrase (see answers below) on the handout sheet so that by the end of the exercise, the basic storyline is available to take home. The "quiz" is not to see how much they know about the story of Gideon; they likely know very little. Instead, it is a way to introduce the story and get familiar with it.

1. **When we first meet Gideon, the eventual hero of our story, he is:**
   Answer: **c.** hiding in a wine press for fear of the enemy (correct).
2. **Gideon is spoken to by:**
   c. an angel (correct).
3. **When told that the Lord is with him and that he is a mighty man of valor, Gideon:**
   a. wonders just where the Lord is now, thank you (correct).
4. **After he is assured that the Lord will deliver the enemy into the hands of the Israelites, Gideon asks for this sign:**
   b. to have dew settle on a fleece of wool (correct).
5. **The enemies of the Israelites had an enormous amount of troops. God's response was to:**
   c. send most of Gideon's troops home (correct).
6. **At the crucial moment in the battle, Gideon and his army:**
   a. break jars, blow trumpets, and shout really loudly (correct).
7. **When they heard all the noise, the enemy:**
   c. panicked and began to fight one another (correct).

KEY CHARACTERISTICS OF ISRAEL'S HOLY WARS

- Israel was a theocracy—with God as the functioning head of government.

- Israel went to war only when God specifically directed, against whom God directed, and the way God directed. When they didn't, the results were often disastrous.

- Israel was instructed by God to intentionally seek military inferiority so that when they went to war they would be dependent on God's miraculous intervention to give them victory.

Eddy Hall,
Decide for Peace

Summarize the story and then lead the group in a discussion of it:

- *Does this seem like a normal battle plan to you?*
- *Why did God make most of the Israelite soldiers go home before the battle? How did this increase the Israelites' trust in God?*
- *Why did God want to make sure that people didn't give themselves credit for the victory?*

Explain that this is what is known as a *holy war*; that is, a battle in which God causes the victory and the people actually do very little real fighting. Holy wars in the ancient scriptures usually required the Israelites to trust God in a radical way. To be faithful meant to rely solely on God's hand—and not on oneself or one's military superiority. Ask: *In what ways is this different from the way nations do battle today? When the Israelites heard the story of Gideon, what do you think it meant to them? Do you think God rescues us anytime we're in a difficult situation? If not, why do we bother to put our trust in God?*

Remind the group of the three key characteristics of Israelite warfare on the sidebar on the previous page. Then do this check-test: *Do our country's policies about war meet the three key standards of ancient Israelite holy war? Which of the following is true for our country?*

- *Is our country a theocracy, with God as the head of government?*
- *Does our nation go to war only when God specifically directs, against whom God directs, and the way God directs?*
- *Does our country intentionally seek military inferiority so that when we go to war we will be dependent on God's miraculous intervention to give us victory?*

Can you think of any nation in the world that meets these standards? (**Note:** Modern-day Israel does not define itself as a theocracy, but as a secular democracy.)

4. APPLY 15 minutes

In the Hebrew Bible, stories told to build faith and trust in God sometimes relied on a context of war or battle. What are *other* kinds of stories we tell that would also demonstrate trust in God? What other kinds of crises? Have the group think about it for a minute before responding: *If you were to tell a story about how God was there for someone (maybe you), what would it be?* Then proceed with one of the following options:

>> **Option A:** Invite someone from the parish to tell the group about a time when they have had to put their trust in God. For instance: someone who was took part in a peace movement and risked imprisonment; someone who endured a life crisis of some kind; someone who has met people who were in extreme need or a traumatic situation, and yet demonstrated great faith; someone who gave up financial security in order to trust God more.

>> **Option B:** Have a group member tell the following story:

The people of southern Sudan have been at war for much of the past 60 years. The government of the country, located in the north of Sudan, regularly bombs and attacks the people of the south. This is partly because of religious differences, as the northern government is run by Muslim extremists who think the southerners, mostly Christians, should convert to Islam. There are also racial and economic factors.

Hundreds of thousands of people have been killed in the fighting and because of the disruption it has caused. Thousands (maybe as many as 2 million) more have fled their homes to become refugees.

"For Christians, nonviolence is not merely tactical behavior but a person's way of being, the attitude of one who is *so convinced of God's love and power* that he or she is not afraid to tackle evil with the weapons of love and truth alone. Love of one's enemy constitutes the nucleus of the 'Christian revolution.'"

Pope Benedict XVI

One such refugee is Rebekah Lueth, the leader of the women's group in a huge refugee camp. When a group of American Christians came to visit her; she spoke for the women. She said: "Why have you come here when I am near my end? Every day I hear the planes flying over head to go to Somalia, where they have a war of a few months. We have been at war 28 years, and why hasn't the world noticed? Is it because of the color of our skin? (Sudanese consider themselves black Africans, while the Somalis are lighter skinned.) All of my agemates have died—most of them. The children have died or been taken into slavery by the Arabs in the north. I do not hate the Muslims, just what their government is doing to us. After all, aren't we all children of one mother; children of the same God? At Christmas I prayed for God to save me. And now you are here. Is this why you have come?"

A few months after this, the refugee camp Rebekah was in was overrun by government troops, and she and the others had to flee to yet another place. Ask: *Where is God for Rebekah? She seems to have great trust in God. Do you think her trust in God is deeper than ours? Why? Why do we not have to trust God to the same degree that someone like Rebekah does? In what ways does God respond to her trust? How would it have felt to have been in the group when Rebekah said, "At Christmas I prayed for God to save me. Is this why you have come?" In what ways are we responsible for the trust people put in God?*

LOOK AHEAD

Next session is about power, who has it, how it is used, and what our responsibility is when it is misused and violence is done to innocent people.

5. RESPOND 10 minutes

Say something like: *On the eve of a big battle, the Israelites had to give up the "security" of weapons and soldiers in order to trust God more. We all know Linus had a blanket for his security. What might it be for you? Your fists? A sport you're really good at? Living in an industrialized country? Pills? A gun? Money? Medical insurance?* Invite participants to name something they use or have that helps them feel safe and secure, and write it in the space at the bottom of the second handout sheet, under **Where's your security?**

Optional: Pass out pieces of towel or fabric (symbolizing a security blanket), and have everyone pin their "security" on it. Invite them to keep the towel until they're really ready to throw away their reliance on what's on that paper, in favor of trusting God.

Close with this prayer or one of your own choosing:

God, we want to turn our security over to you, so that we can rely on you more. Please don't let us down, and show us plainly how you are there for us. Amen.

# INSIGHTS FROM SCRIPTURE

The story of Gideon is a clear challenge to modern attitudes about fighting and war. In a situation where God's people were desperately in need of liberation, God didn't allow the Israelites to use the normal "tools" for fighting; instead their primary weapons were their faith in God and their ability to put this into practice in unsettling situations.

As the book of Judges reveals, the conquest of Canaan did not happen overnight or without difficulty. The peoples inhabiting the land prior to the arrival of the Israelites were firmly entrenched and were not to be easily pushed aside by these new arrivals. What they may not have counted on was the presence among these immigrants of Yahweh, the God of Israel, whose purposes were being worked out through this people.

As the story opens (around 1150 B.C.E.), Gideon was living in fear of the Midianites, the dominant group in the area. Evidently the Midianites exacted taxes from the Israelites in the form of levies against the grain harvest. For the Israelite peasant, this would have been particularly oppressive, because for them, as for all agrarian peoples, access to the land and its fruits was crucial for survival.

When Gideon learned that he would be the one to deliver Israel from their oppressors, he was understandably skeptical. As the story develops, his skepticism might well have increased; instead of providing Gideon with more troops and armaments, the Lord required that Gideon *reduce* the size of his army. Why? "Israel would only take the credit away from me, saying, 'My own hand has delivered me.'" God wanted it to be clear that it was not through their own power, but through the power of the Lord that the battle would be won.

When many in our day turn to the Hebrew Bible to substantiate warfare as a legitimate undertaking for people of faith, they also want to parley this into support for large military build-ups. The story of Gideon makes clear that warfare for Israel was not a matter of the latest technology or numerical strength; in fact, these were specifically repudiated as inappropriate. To be faithful meant to rely solely on God's hand—and not on oneself or one's military superiority.

This story still does not completely answer the difficult questions of God's involvement in battle, but it does give a clear view of how God's people are to live and to deal with their enemies—by faith.

The Saga of Gideon's Battle (Judges 6–7)

In Real Life
Exploring tough questions facing youth today

1. **When we first meet Gideon, the eventual hero of our story, he is:**
   a. standing on a mountain praying to God.
   b. lying on his back, having been struck blind and knocked off his horse by God.
   c. hiding in a wine press for fear of the enemy.

2. **Gideon is spoken to by:**
   a. Moses.
   b. Jesus.
   c. an angel.

3. **When told that the Lord is with him and that he is a mighty man of valor, Gideon:**
   a. wonders just where the Lord is now, thank you.
   b. sets off to rescue his people in a golden chariot.
   c. signs a contract to be spokesman for a major supplier of athletic sandals.

4. **After he is assured that the Lord will deliver the enemy into the hands of the Israelites, Gideon asks for this sign:**
   a. to see a large, glowing star in the heavens.
   b. to have dew settle on a fleece of wool.
   c. that a stranger will meet him and whisper the secret codeword.

5. **The enemies of the Israelites had an enormous amount of troops. God's response was to:**
   a. call for reinforcements.
   b. provide Gideon with supernatural weapons.
   c. send most of Gideon's troops home.

6. **At the crucial moment in the battle, Gideon and his army:**
   a. break jars, blow trumpets, and shout really loudly.
   b. lose their nerve and retreat.
   c. are reinforced by the Amalekites, enabling them to overcome the enemy.

7. **When they heard all the noise, the enemy:**
   a. wondered if this was a new band from Seattle.
   b. laughed so hard they couldn't fight.
   c. panicked and began to fight one another.

God Is a Warrior? : Session 2

Permission is granted to photocopy this handout for use with this session.

Holy War?

In Real Life — Exploring tough questions facing youth today

Key characteristics of Israel's holy wars:
- Israel was a theocracy—with God as the functioning head of government.
- Israel went to war only when God specifically directed, against whom God directed, and the way God directed. When they didn't the results were often disastrous.
- Israel was instructed by God to intentionally seek military inferiority so that when they went to war they would be dependent on God's miraculous intervention to give them victory.

from Eddy Hall's Decide for Peace

Where's your security?

On the eve of a big battle, the Israelites had to give up the "security" of weapons and soldiers in order to trust God more.

What would **you** have to give up reliance on in order to trust God more? In the space below, write something you use or have that helps you feel safe and secure. For Linus it was a blanket! What might it be for you? Your fists? A sport you're really good at? Living in an industrialized country? Pills? A gun? Money? Medical insurance?

God Is a Warrior? : Session 2

Permission is granted to photocopy this handout for use with this session.

Exploring tough questions facing youth today

>>> **SESSION 3**

A ROOM WITH A VIEW >>>

>> KEY VERSE

But Naboth said to Ahab, "The Lord forbid that I should give you my ancestral inheritance." (1 Kings 21:3)

>> FAITH STORY

1 Kings 21:1-19

>> FAITH FOCUS

This story depicts another kind of violence in the Bible, and God's response to it. After King David and King Solomon, Israel divided into two nation-states, and Israelite leaders were often guilty of apostasy—worshiping the other gods of the land. When Israel's leaders were unjust, violence resulted, along with the kind of excesses warned of in the book of Deuteronomy (cf. chapter 17:14ff.). How did God react? Does God fight for the innocent? The story of Naboth prompts us to decide what we will do when weaker members of society suffer at the hands of unscrupulous leaders.

>> SESSION GOAL

Help participants formulate a response when violence is done to innocent people.

>> Materials needed and advance preparation

- Chalkboard/chalk or newsprint/marker
- Handout sheet for Session 3 (an abbreviated version of the United Nations' *Universal Declaration of Human Rights*)
- Bibles
- Stack of recent newspapers or magazines, scissors (*Option* in Apply)
- Media player; Internet access (*Option* in Apply)
- Research current unjust situations in your country (Respond)

TEACHING PLAN

1. FOCUS 5 minutes

This session is about power, who has it, how it is used, and what our responsibility is when it is misused and violence is done to innocent people.

Have an arm-wrestling, thumb-wrestling, or leg-wrestling contest. When you've declared a winner, announce that the winner now has the right to order everyone else to do something (like sit in a corner, sit on the floor, stand on one foot, or sit on an imaginary chair with backs to the wall). If you are outside, the winner could take everyone else's coats or shoes. The idea is to give the winner some kind of power over the others.

2. CONNECT 10 minutes

While still under the authority of the wrestling contest winner, have the group vote on the following propositions. Record the vote tallies ("yea" or "nay") on newsprint, chalkboard, or a notepad. Briefly discuss the group's response to each statement.

Proposition A: People in power are generally there because they've exhibited good leadership skills.

Proposition B: People get what they deserve in this world; if you lead a good life, you will generally prosper and be happy.

Proposition C: Faith in God is the best way to spare yourself and your family injury or catastrophe.

Proposition D: If a group of people is being ill-treated or exploited anywhere in the world, we have a responsibility to try to do something about it.

3. EXPLORE THE BIBLE 15 minutes

Announce that the wrestling ruler's time of power is up, and allow people to take their seats or retrieve their belongings.

Distribute copies of the abbreviated version of the United Nations' *Universal Declaration of Human Rights* (on the handout sheet). Have everyone briefly look it over.

Next, read aloud the story of Naboth's vineyard (1 Kings 21:1-19). If you have enough people, divide into parts: a narrator, the king (a spoiled rich man), Naboth (honest and sincere), Queen Jezebel (scheming and ruthless), two scoundrels (willing to do anything for the right price), and God.

Following the reading, have the participants look through the rights listed as part of the *Universal Declaration*. Say: *Which of Naboth's rights were violated? Call out the number of the right and read it aloud.*

Lead a group discussion:

- *Why was this parcel of land of such value to Naboth?*
- *Why didn't the king respect this?*
- *Name and list the characters in this drama. What role did each of them play? How did the various characters fail God's call for justice and fairness (the king and queen; the elders and nobles; the "people"; the false witnesses)?*
- *Why did no one stand up in Naboth's defense?*
- *Although King Ahab might have thought he had gotten away with taking the vineyard, did his deed go unnoticed? Is there "justice" for those who abuse others for their own gain? For those who are abused?*
- *What was Elijah's role in this drama?*

PLACES WHERE ANCESTRAL LANDS AND TRADITIONS ARE FALLING TO POWERFUL INTERESTS:

- The invasion of rainforests by logging companies and settlers
- American culture overwhelming the cultures of many of the world's people as it is exported via satellite
- The ongoing situation of aboriginal peoples, most of whom live in poverty and struggle to retain traditional ways of life
- Multinational corporations controlling large tracts of land in nations that are struggling economically

4. APPLY 10 minutes

Help participants think of situations where someone has had their traditions or their valued lands taken over by more powerful interests. List situations on the board or newsprint. (See sidebar for examples - don't forget the European conquest of the New World and the destruction of the Native Americans way of life.)

Choose one situation in which the interests of a weaker party are being overrun by a more powerful group or agency (preferably one in which your country, or interests in your country, have played a part.)

Options: Invite participants to collect stories of this type. They may have to read a little between the lines. Have a stack of recent newspapers or news magazines on hand, along with scissors, or do a brief Web search if you have Internet access. Explore together the video (about 2 minutes) and movement called Charter for Compassion https://charterforcompassion.org/charter/charter-overvew.

Ask: *Why has the more powerful party chosen to violate the weaker one in this way? Does the weaker party have a choice in the matter? Why does God "allow" some people to be abused by others? If youth were concerned about this situation, what could be done to oppose or change it?*

LOOK AHEAD

For next session, prepare yourself for some "violence" from the New Testament! For this, you'll need to prepare two people for the "disrupter" scene in Explore.

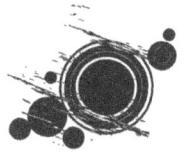

5. RESPOND 10 minutes

Go over the list again, and this time help participants name the person they would talk to, if they were a prophet like Elijah, calling the "powers" to responsibility. Would it be a president or CEO of a company?

Contact your diocesan peace and justice office (or a group like Amnesty International) to find out about a situation in the world or in your nation where a group or individual is being treated unjustly. Contact information is in the resources section of the unit introduction. Ask for the chance to make an announcement at the weekend masses to inform the congregation about this situation and invite them to respond in prayer and in action. Write letters, e-mails, or use social media to express to the appropriate authorities your concerns about this situation.

OR

After getting the facts about an unjust situation involving a corporation, begin an educational campaign to help other youth in the community understand the issues involved. (For instance, a popular clothing store has recently been criticized for employing cheap labor in Central America in producing the clothes it sells.) What action would be appropriate?

Look again at the vote taken at the beginning of the session. How do the participants feel about how they voted? Would they change their votes in any way following today's discussion?

INSIGHTS FROM SCRIPTURE

The story of Naboth's vineyard is a fascinating and disturbing character study. Naboth was a common man living on his ancestral land. He could not give up this land, because it was part of his family inheritance; as such, it was entrusted to his care by the Lord. It was his only means of supporting himself and his family. On the other hand, there was King Ahab, who coveted this nearby parcel of land for a vegetable garden. When he discovered that Naboth would not sell him this land—indeed, that he could not—he engaged in something of a royal pout. In this story we see why Queen Jezebel's name has forever been associated with treachery, as she encouraged the king to use his power without mercy or a sense of justice. The people in the story—the elders and nobles and the ordinary citizens—were taken into this web of deceit with disturbing ease.

In many ways, it's the same old story of those in power using the means of power to get whatever they want from whomever they want. It is a very disturbing story, as a leader of God's people is party to the treachery that ends the life of another of God's people.

The modern parallels of this story are at our fingertips: governments abusing their power to exert or gain control, corporations exercising their financial and political power to overwhelm individuals and groups that stand in their way. The forces of modern life—technology, militarism, consumerism—threaten to inundate the lives of real people.

What Ahab and Jezebel forgot, as we often do, is that such deeds do not go unnoticed. The Lord is an ever-present witness to even those schemes hatched behind closed palace or corporate doors. Though God's justice did not prevent heinous acts as this one against Naboth, this justice can and will be evident in the long run—so long as there are faithful people like Elijah to speak out against it.

Universal Declaration of Human Rights (abbreviated version)

Now, therefore, THE GENERAL ASSEMBLY proclaims this Universal Declaration of Human Rights as a common standard of achievement for all peoples and all nations, to the end that every individual and every organ of society, keeping this Declaration constantly in mind, shall strive by teaching and education to promote respect for these rights and freedoms....

ARTICLE 1—Right to equality.
ARTICLE 2—Freedom from discrimination.
ARTICLE 3—Right to life, liberty, personal security.
ARTICLE 4—Freedom from slavery.
ARTICLE 5—Freedom from torture, degrading treatment.
ARTICLE 6—Right to recognition as a person before the law.
ARTICLE 7—Right to equality before the law.
ARTICLE 8—Right to remedy by competent tribunal.
ARTICLE 9—Freedom from arbitrary arrest, exile.
ARTICLE 10—Right to fair public hearing.
ARTICLE 11—Right to be considered innocent until proven guilty.
ARTICLE 12—Freedom from interference with privacy, family, home, correspondence.
ARTICLE 13—Right to free movement in and out of any country.
ARTICLE 14—Right to asylum in other countries from persecution.
ARTICLE 15—Right to a nationality and freedom to change it.
ARTICLE 16—Right to marriage and family.
ARTICLE 17—Right to own property.
ARTICLE 18—Freedom of belief and religion.
ARTICLE 19—Freedom of opinion and information.
ARTICLE 20—Right of peaceful assembly and association.
ARTICLE 21—Right to participate in government, and in free elections.
ARTICLE 22—Right to social security.
ARTICLE 23—Right to desirable work and to join trade unions.
ARTICLE 24—Right to rest and leisure.
ARTICLE 25—Right to adequate living standard.
ARTICLE 26—Right to education.
ARTICLE 27—Right to participate in the cultural life of community.
ARTICLE 28—Right to social order assuring human rights.
ARTICLE 29—Community duties essential to free and full development.
ARTICLE 30—Freedom from State or personal interference in the above rights.

Explore the video and movement called Charter for Compassion.

(CharterForCompassion.org)

Adopted by the General Assembly
United Nations
December 10, 1948

Permission is granted to photocopy this handout for use with this session.

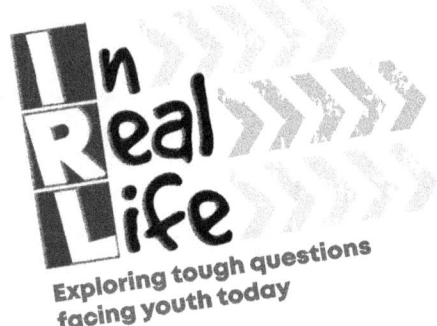

>>> SESSION 4

CLEANING HOUSE >>>

>> KEY VERSE

He was teaching and saying, "Is it not written, 'My house shall be called a house of prayer for all the nations'? But you have made it a den of robbers." (Mark 11:17)

>> FAITH STORY

Mark 11:15-19

>> FAITH FOCUS

In a fit of explosive anger, Jesus drove the money-changers and sellers of pigeons out of the Temple. While Jesus had on other occasions used very strong language in condemning the religious practices of others, this is the only story in the Gospels that indicates he used physical force to make his point. What does this action of Jesus mean for us, who try to follow his way?

>> SESSION GOAL

Help participants clarify the difference between forceful prophetic actions and violent ones.

>> Materials needed and advance preparation

- Prepare two people for the "disrupter" scene (see Explore).
- Bibles
- A variety of "religious" items: pictures, bookmarks, pins, etc., and a small table for displaying them (see Explore)
- Chalkboard/chalk or newsprint/marker
- Candles for each person, matches (*Option B* in Respond)
- Copies of the handout sheet for Session 4 (*Option C* in Respond)

TEACHING PLAN

1. & 2. FOCUS/CONNECT 10-15 minutes

Engage the group in a values continuum. Have them stand at one end or the other of the room, or somewhere in between, based on whether they agree with or disagree with the following propositions. Discuss the group's responses to each one briefly before moving on to the next one.

1. It is a sin to be angry with another person.
2. If you're really angry with someone, you should tell them about it.
3. There are times when sufficient anger could justify violence against another person or group of people, especially if you know you are right.
4. Read the sidebar about "gospel mayhem," and ask if they agree with such actions.
5. When Jesus turned over the tables of the money-changers in the Temple and drove out those selling sacrificial animals, he was acting violently.

> ### GOSPEL MAYHEM
>
> "They're messy revolutionaries. They pour blood on missiles and don't clean it up. They hammer nose cones and don't pick up the pieces. When they go to court some are so ornery they turn their backs to the judge.... Atlantic Life Community has been sustained ... because its faith in nonviolence is grounded in the Word. The prophets and Jesus determine the action: swords into plowshares, disruption in the temple, the way of the Suffering Servant and the cross.... [It's] gospel mayhem in the system."
>
> Excerpted from "Gospel Mayhem," by Jim Douglass, *Sojourners*

3. EXPLORE THE BIBLE 15-20 minutes

Shift to this activity by saying: *How do you determine when someone is acting violently and when they are being prophetic in a forceful way? And what's a loving Jesus doing shouting and overturning tables?*

Distribute Bibles, and have a group member read the story of Jesus driving out the money-changers and those who sold animals for sacrifice (Mark 11:15-19).

Disrupter scene: On a table, have some religious symbols or other "church stuff" for sale. Have one person "hawking" these wares. "Get your pictures of Jesus right here! Striking resemblance! Guaranteed to bring a blessing to any room where it hangs—hang it in yours and don't be surprised if your grades improve! The latest in 14-carat gold crosses! Don't leave home without one!"

Have another person prepared to disrupt this retail operation. The scene is replayed four different times, with the "disrupter" using a different method of disruption each time. After each incident, **have the group decide whether the method employed violence** in achieving its objective. You as leader may need to decide whether the term "violence" needs to be defined before you start.

The four different methods are:

1. matter-of-factly sweeping the items off the table, calling for this kind of crass commercialism to be banned from the church property;
2. overturning the table, angrily denouncing the sale of merchandise;
3. calling the merchant a greedy fool, telling him/her to take this despicable business elsewhere, turning over the table;
4. all of the above, plus pushing the merchant out of the room.

Was there a point that the actions of the "disrupter" became violent? When was this? What made it so?

Ask the group if this scene, one of the few stories about Jesus recorded in three of the four Gospels, is in keeping with Jesus' behavior in other stories about him in the Bible. How is it similar? How is it different?

Jesus' actions are very strong here. When attempting to address an unjust or immoral situation, how do we draw the line between *forceful* actions and *violent* actions? **Make a list** of the criteria for keeping an action showing disapproval of the actions of others from becoming violent.

4. APPLY 10 minutes

When can actions such as Jesus' actions in this story be important or even necessary in addressing a situation where something is wrong? What purpose do such actions serve?

If your government was doing something you didn't think was right, for instance, refusing to fully fund public schools, scaling back environmental regulations to allow transport of toxic waste, or pushing through permits to expand industrial areas in productive farmland, would you...

- be willing to write a letter to a government official about it?
- march in a demonstration in protest?
- stand in front of the government office building singing and praying with other protesters when the government workers arrived Monday morning?

- enter the office and refuse to leave until the person in charge came to speak to you?
- ask for the records pertaining to the issue and dump them in the street as a symbolic act of protest?

Can the group think of other people through history who have carried out acts like Jesus' cleansing the Temple to call attention to a situation? (Examples include: Wikileaks whistleblowers, Women in Black, regular witnesses at School of the Americas, Idle No More protesters.) Were their actions widely supported at the time? In the long run, did their actions help change things for the better? Is it important to consider whether an action will really change a situation, or should some things be done no matter what?

What if your *church* were doing something you felt was wrong? Would you change any of your tactics? Why or why not? (Keep in mind that Jesus' actions were calling out injustices perpetrated by religious authorities.)

5. RESPOND 5-10 minutes

>> **Option A:** As a group, write a psalm-prayer asking God to give us the courage to stand for what we believe in, but to do so without hatred or violence.

>> **Option B:** Light candles as symbols of hope and strength, and raise them high as you close with a prayer that each of us will have the courage to act on our convictions should there be a situation that merits our action.

>> **Option C:** Have five readers close the session by reading "Time to Take Off" (handout sheet).

INSIGHTS FROM SCRIPTURE

The story of the cleansing of the Temple is one of the most intriguing texts in the New Testament, in part because it stands somewhat alone; there are no other instances of Jesus acting in quite this way. There is another facet to this intrigue. Jesus' actions here stretch our understanding of him. If we wish to characterize Jesus as the meek and gentle savior, the sight of him running the money-changers out of the Temple with shouts of anger pushes us to see another side of him. Therefore, what are we, who want to be like Jesus, called to *do*?

In cleansing the Temple, Jesus stood in the tradition of the Hebrew prophets who often emphasized their teachings in public, symbolic ways (i.e., Jeremiah placing the yoke around his neck; Hosea taking a prostitute as his wife). Jesus also used physical deeds to highlight his message; for instance, he referred to himself as the "bread of life" after feeding the multitudes, and he healed the paralytic to show that he had authority to forgive sins.

>>>
LOOK AHEAD

If you plan to have a "prophet" visit for Session 6, consider now whom you might ask.

>>>
"Nonviolence is sometimes taken to mean surrender, lack of involvement and passivity, but this is not the case... The decisive and consistent practice of nonviolence has produced impressive results."

Pope Francis
Message for World Day of Peace 2017

⟫⟫⟫ WAGING PEACE

For more examples of nonviolent direct action for peace and justice, see Quaker David Hartsough's <u>Waging Peace: Global Adventures of a Lifelong Activist.</u>

⟫ RIGHTEOUS ANGER

The money-changers and pigeon-sellers really aroused Jesus' righteous anger. Their job, accepted (even encouraged) by the religious authorities, was to change the Roman currency into Jewish coinage that could be presented in the Temple. The pigeons were sold to the poor people who needed to offer them for sacrifice. (The well-off could afford to bring their own sheep or goats to sacrifice.) The exchange rates exploited the poor and the requirement that people buy animals to sacrifice to atone for their sins or to prove their holiness allowed the priestly class to make money at the expense of the common people. Jesus was incensed at the perversion of worship that these practices fostered. While Jesus had on other occasions used very strong language to condemn the religious practices of others, this is the only story in the Gospels that indicates he used physical force to make his point.

The question of using forceful actions to make one's point has been a challenging one for people of faith through the centuries. On the one hand, some people have quite often been willing to fight and kill for one cause or another—often lifting high the banner of Christ at the same time. On the other hand, many believers are quite reluctant to be "disruptive" by overtly challenging institutions that are unjust in our own society.

Jesus presented a "third way," as theologian Walter Wink terms it—a way that seizes moral initiative, refuses to fear the old order and its rules, and exposes the injustice of a system.

People who want to be peacemakers continue to struggle to find their way through these questions as well. While some have actively challenged what they perceive to be unjust governmental or social practices, others have been reluctant to challenge institutions (secular or religious) either out of their respect for authority or unwillingness to be confrontive.

⟫ CONDEMNING INJUSTICE ON BOTH SIDES OF CONFLICT

Forceful action for change is a pertinent issue for our time as well as in Jesus' time. Some see the use of military force in the service of humanitarian interests as quite appropriate. Others want the faithful to confront unjust structures and activities. Still others strive to be "separate from the world" by keeping their involvement in governments or social institutions to a minimum, even avoiding voting as well as military service.

How should people of faith challenge a policy or practice that is unfair or unethical, especially if it is religious in nature? When we do issue such a challenge? Can we go too far in our actions, demeaning or harming in some way those with whom we disagree? Dare we try to follow Jesus in this as well?

Like Jesus and the biblical prophets, a person who speaks for God often has to condemn injustice on *both* sides of a conflict. While the language, even the actions, might need to be forceful (not violent) to call attention to injustice, calling people to right actions is an important part of making peace.

Time to Take Off

A Rendition of Isaiah 40:28-31
by David Radcliff

In Real Life — Exploring tough questions facing youth today

Reader: Have you not known? Have you not heard?
1: Hear? Know? We hear and know so much—too much!
2: More than we want to know; more than we can stand to hear!
3: Who do you know? Did you hear that?
4: Hear what? Know who?

Reader: The Lord is the everlasting God, the creator of the ends of the earth.
4: So that's who.
3: So who's that?
1: So that's who created this mess!
2: So that's who can get us out of this mess....

Reader: God gives power to the faint, and strengthens the powerless.
3: Power Rangers; power player; power hitter
1: Military power; political power; economic power.
ALL: The ones that need the power never get it.
4: Power to give; power to love; power to try
2: Power to stand; power to live; power to fly

Reader: Those who wait for the Lord shall renew their strength, they shall mount up with wings like eagles;
1: Give me wings to fly away from this place!
4: Give me wings to get where I want to go in life!
ALL: Gimme, gimme, gimme—is that what wings are for?!
2: *(after slight pause)* Give me wings to see the earth and all its people.
3: Give me wings to go where you want me to go in life, Lord.

Reader: They shall run and not be weary, they shall walk and not faint.
1: God gives us the power
2: to stand with those without power
3: to stand with power for what we believe in
4: to have the power to live and achieve
ALL: whatever God wants us to be.
4: Stand!
3: Run!
2: Live!
1: Fly!

God Is a Warrior? : Session 4

Permission is granted to photocopy this handout for use with this session.

Exploring tough questions facing youth today

>>> **SESSION 5**

WHEN YOU WANT TO HIT BACK >>>

>> KEY VERSE

When his disciples James and John saw [that the Samaritans did not receive him], they said, "Lord, do you want us to command fire to come down from heaven and consume them?" (Luke 9:54)

>> FAITH STORY

Luke 9:51-56

>> FAITH FOCUS

The willingness to destroy others who anger or threaten us is a disturbing facet of being human. In this episode, even Jesus' disciples showed that they were not immune to this tendency, as they wondered aloud whether they should destroy a village of Samaritans who had rejected them and Jesus. While Jesus rebuked them, they nonetheless showed that even within the inner circle of Jesus' followers, there was an active spirit of violence.

>> SESSION GOAL

Help participants formulate a nonviolent response when angry, even if violence seems justified.

TEACHING PLAN

>> Materials needed and advance preparation

- Large sticky notes
- Felt marker
- Newsprint/markers or chalkboard/chalk
- Long chalkboard/chalk or strip of paper 1-2 meters (3 to 6 feet) long (Focus)
- Copies of the handout sheets for Session 5
- Writing paper and pencils
- Bibles
- Ronald Sider's book *Nonviolence, The Invincible Weapon?* or David Hartsough's *Waging Peace: Global Adventures of a Lifelong Activist* (Option B in Apply)

1. FOCUS 10 minutes

Ask the group, *What are some different motives people have for fighting?* Answers can include why people fight wars as well as why individuals fight with each other. As each answer is given, write it with a marker—in one word, if possible—on a sticky note. Attach the sticky notes randomly on a chalkboard or newsprint.

Next draw a line, 1-2 meters (3-6 feet) long, across the top of a chalkboard or on a strip of paper mounted on the wall. Label the left end of this line **SELFISH/MEAN**. Label the right end **SELFLESS/NOBLE**. Explain, *Some reasons people fight are totally selfish*. Then ask, *What would be one example of a self-centered reason to fight?* As the group agrees on one of the most contemptible reasons for fighting (for example, to retaliate against someone who has hurt them), take the sticky note that has that motive written on it and attach it to the continuum clear at the "selfish" end.

EXPLORE NONVIOLENCE

Based on the teachings of Jesus and Gandhi, Pace e Bene offers a variety of tranings on nonviolence. (http://PaceEBene.org/trainings-and-speakers). The trainings cover both the powerful vision and the practical tools of nonviolence.

Then say, *Some reasons people fight are selfless. What would be an example of a noble reason people might fight?* Attach the motive the group chooses (to defend the powerless and innocent, for example) to the "selfless" end of the scale. If none of your notes has a selfless motive on it, ask the group to come up with one.

Next, ask the group where along the scale they would place the motive of self-defense. (Probably somewhere between the two extremes.) Then have the group decide, one by one, where each of the motives should be placed along the scale, until all have been ranked. If other motives are suggested during the ranking, add those as well.

2. CONNECT 10 minutes

Engage the group in a "what if" exercise. Distribute copies of the first handout sheet and pencils, and ask them to write short endings to the statements under "Threatened."

After everyone has had a chance to write, discuss the statements one at a time. Encourage people to explain and support their statements.

3. EXPLORE THE BIBLE 10 minutes

Shift to this activity by saying: *We can think of plenty of times when violence seems justified, or when motives for fighting are selfless and noble, or in defense of someone innocent. In the story we're about to read, Jesus' disciples had good motives* **AND** *biblical precedent for wanting to hit back....*

Have one person read Luke 9:51-54. (Wait to read v. 55 until later.) Explain that it was not uncommon for Samaritans to turn away Jewish travelers who were going to Jerusalem. Do they know why? (The Samaritans and Jews were enemies during this period of history. The Jews despised the Samaritans for several reasons: Although both groups had descended from Abraham, the Jews felt that the Samaritans were not "pure," as they had intermarried with non-Jews; the Samaritans did not see Jerusalem as their holy city, worshiping instead at Mount Gerazim; the Samaritans had gone to war against the Jews decades earlier.)

Ask the group what the disciples wanted to do to this Samaritan village. What is the closest analogy in modern warfare to this image of fire coming down from heaven to destroy a city in its entirety? This may seem like an extreme response to a town that had simply refused to be hospitable to the group. Have the group list the reasons that the disciples might have reacted so strongly and violently. Leave space following each reason to write something later. Include in the list these possibilities:

- Racism may have made the disciples value Samaritan lives less (prejudice + power = racism).
- The Samaritans had turned away Jesus (who, to the disciples, was a very important religious leader), an affront that deserved a swift and severe response.
- The disciples may have felt that as followers of Jesus, they were very powerful people (see 9:1-2, 46).
- They thought that they had the capacity to easily destroy this village with a burst of fire from heaven (having weapons makes one want to use them).
- Their supposed "weapon" (fire from heaven) would have allowed them to kill the people of this village without having to confront them face to face.

4. APPLY 15 minutes

Now ask the group to list a similar contemporary situation beside each of the reasons for fighting given above. For instance, for the willingness to do violence against someone of another race, the brutality of white police officers against people of color could be cited. The ability to kill others without having to confront them personally is available through modern weapons such as air strikes. For our willingness to harm others because of religious differences, the Crusades of the Middle Ages or modern prejudice against Jews or Muslims could be named. In other words, *In what ways do we fall into the same trap as the disciples in our use of violence against others? What did Jesus do to challenge people to think differently about enemies?*

Now read verse 55 of Luke 9, noting how Jesus "rebuked" the disciples. This is the same strong word used to describe Jesus' casting out of demons. Then continue with one of the options below.

 Option A: Distribute copies of the second handout sheet: "Operation Desert Rescue." Tell the group that after reading through this scenario, their task will be to imagine ways that the situation can be changed to help people see their enemies in a more humane way. Read the scenario aloud as others follow along.

Either break into groups of three (each group dealing with one or two questions), or work as a whole group to think of ways the Katestan situation could be defused. Keep notes of the group's work.

>> **Option B: Strategy session**
Think of the last time your country was at war, or had troops fighting somewhere. What were some of the issues involved? Who was involved? Who "started" the war, and why? Who or what was in danger or threatened? What kind of oppression was involved?

After you've remembered the context of this war, form groups of four (if you have a large group) and **draw up a list** of specific actions people of faith could take as a group, using only nonviolent, spiritual weapons to fight that war. After a few minutes, ask the groups to report on the ideas they have come up with.

They may not come up with much. If so, this is probably because we are so influenced by our dominant culture that we tend not to even be aware of options for dealing with military oppression or threats that are not themselves based on coercive power.

You may want to ask, *Are you aware of situations where military force has been successfully overcome by nonviolent means?* Invite participants to share stories. You might mention examples from either Ronald Sider's *Non-violence, The Invincible Weapon?* or David Hartsough's *Waging Peace: Global Adventures of a Lifelong Activist*. See also resources in this unit's introduction.

Explain that in a short session like this, you can barely scratch the surface of the subject of spiritual weapons, but that you will look at two or three spiritual weapons as examples.

The Counterattack of Love
An enemy, as Jesus uses the word, is not necessarily someone you dislike, but rather someone who hates you or seeks to harm you. If your enemy's attempt to hurt you (or your nation) is an aggressive attack, loving your enemy is Jesus' way of counterattacking. The unique thing about this spiritual weapon—the counterattack of love—is that the only time you can use it is when someone has harmed you or is wanting to harm you. Your enemy's attack, or intended attack, creates an opening for this powerful spiritual weapon.

>>>

"Even when a person's motives were unselfish, Jesus expressed disapproval of violence. When something truly terrible is happening and something needs to be done about it, what are followers of Jesus to do? Just stand by passively and helplessly? Hardly. Jesus calls us to engage the fight with evil just as vigorously as he did–using the weapons he used: a counterattack of love, prophetic witness, intercessory prayer, even giving your own life."

Eddy Hall,
Decide for Peace

›››
COUNTER-ATTACK WITH A GUITAR

Have you heard the extraordinary story of Ted Studebaker? Watch a short video on YouTube (search for "Ted Studebaker ABC News Story"). He was a young Brethren man who could not conscientiously accept military service in Vietnam, but was perfectly willing to go—not with weapons but with a guitar and an idea that tools can accomplish more than guns.

Ted's story consists of his agricultural work with the mountain people at Di Linh, of his wedding to another volunteer, and of his martyrdom two weeks later on April 26, 1971, when the Viet Cong invaded the house of the Vietnam Christian Service unit, shooting Ted to death. "Ted Studebaker was a man who believed peace was possible," concluded a news correspondent who broadcast the story. Ted's faithful discipleship took risks, and even welcomed confrontation, engaging in it lovingly. It meant going to war with a guitar, not a gun.

It is not natural to love an enemy; the natural response is to return evil for evil. That gives this weapon much of its power. When you respond in love to someone trying to hurt you, you catch your enemy by surprise. Your enemy wonders, "Why do you respond this way?" This can create an opening for love to dislodge your enemy's hatred and fear.

1. In Luke 6:27, Jesus lists three specific ways to love enemies. What are they?
   a. _____ to those who hate you.
   b. _____ those who curse you.
   c. _____ those who abuse you.

2. What do you think "Do good to those who hate you" means? Does this refer only to an inner attitude, or does it require outward actions?

3. What does it mean to curse someone? Blessing is the opposite of cursing. So what does it mean to bless someone?

4. How do you think Jesus wants us to pray for those who abuse us? What is the difference between praying *for* and praying *at* those who abuse us?

After a few minutes, lead the group through envisioning how people of faith in your country could use the counterattack of love to fight the war you described above. You could also use some of the sidebars to generate ideas ("Counterattack with a Guitar," "Army for Peace").

5. Try to imagine how your country's response would have been different if your nation's leaders had chosen a strategy, not of trying to defeat the enemy, but of launching a counterattack of love.

   a. *Do good to those who hate you.* What were some of the needs of the people in the enemy nation? How could your country have taken the initiative to "do practical acts of kindness" to those people?

   b. *Bless those who curse you.* Did the leaders of your enemy nation call your country names? Say you were evil? Wish for the worst to happen to you? Those are all examples of cursing. What would have happened if the people of your country had responded by looking (however hard you had to look) to find good things to say about the leaders and people of the enemy nation? What if spiritual leaders in your country had called on the faithful across the country to pray for the best possible future for the people and leaders of the enemy nation? What are some of the kind things your country might have said about the enemy nation? What are some of the good things you could have wished/prayed for your nation's enemy?

   c. *Pray for those who abuse you.* It's easy to pray that God will make my abuser stop abusing me. But what would it look like to pray that my abuser will experience the richness of all God has in mind for him or her? Think again of the country your own country was most recently at war with. If you would pray this kind of prayer for that nation, what might it include?

6. Now, try to imagine. If your nation's political leaders and spiritual leaders had made the counterattack of love—doing good to your enemy, blessing your enemy, and praying for your enemy—central to your response to your nation's enemy in the last war:

   a. How might that have changed your nation's mood?
   b. How might it have changed your nation's relationship with the enemy nation?
   c. What difference might it have made in the war?
   d. What difference might it have made in the relationship between the two nations in the aftermath of the war?

Wind up this activity by asking group members to name other spiritual weapons that may be effective in fighting violence. Possible answers include prophetic witness, intercessory prayer, martyrdom, and the power of the faith community's example.

5. RESPOND 5-10 minutes

(If you broke into smaller groups to discuss the Katestan situation, have those groups report on their "solutions." If you worked as a total group, you will already have done this. You are ready to close with prayer.)

Make a point of blessing "enemies" in your prayers—asking God's best for them. Or, use the prayer at the bottom of page 33. **Warning**: It is a difficult prayer to pray, especially if you have a specific group or individual in mind as an enemy.

INSIGHTS FROM SCRIPTURE

In one of the most disturbing scenes from the New Testament, the disciples wondered, maybe even hoped aloud, whether they should wipe out a Samaritan village because they had not received hospitality there. *We* are left wondering how those who have traveled so close to Jesus could consider such an action against others.

It would not have been unusual for a Samaritan village to turn away Jewish travelers heading for Jerusalem. After all, the Jews despised the Samaritans, at least in part because the two groups had chosen different locations for their central place of worship. The very fact that Jesus was on his way to Jerusalem would have been proof enough that he was not the messiah *they* expected. It would likewise have not been unusual for a group of Jewish people who had had a run-in with Samaritans to feel resentment toward them.

When they asked to "call down fire" on the village, James and John, a.k.a. "Sons of Thunder," seemed to be living up to their dramatic name. But they also knew their scriptures. They were referring to a passage in 2 Kings 1:10, 12 in which the great prophet of God, Elijah, twice called down fire on soldiers who came to escort him to the Samaritan king. These disciples had religious and historical precedent for their response! But Jesus rebuked this spirit of vengeance, saying, in effect, I bring a new way, a new spirit of saving life, not destroying it.

This session furthermore probes a more troubling side of human nature—what is it that causes us to make the leap from angry thoughts to unrestrained violence? What will we do about it? In what situations is our anger appropriate? When do we risk going too far in our response to others who have provoked us? What role do racism, religious prejudice, or other stereotypes play in this process?

In other places (particularly the Sermon on the Mount), Jesus provided clear guidelines for our treatment of others, especially those who mistreat or anger us. He taught love and forgiveness, along with the refusal to judge others as evil. These attitudes are some of Jesus' most distinguishing teachings. As such, they provide a clear challenge to what others consider acceptable behavior.

In this story, Jesus clearly and promptly condemned the disciples' violent tendencies. In what ways does our faith in Jesus move us away from violence and toward more responsible, more respectful and more Christ-like reactions to those who offend us or who would do us harm? Even when violence is used in what seems to be a good cause, Jesus preached and embodied a message of love, forgiveness, and the willingness to suffer violence rather than to inflict it.

LOOK AHEAD

If you plan to use the extender session, next time would be the time to do it. Two of the options call for viewing movies: *Gandhi* or *Dead Man Walking*. Make plans for the equipment and place to show the movie.

If you're going on to Session 6, recruit a "visiting prophet," and brief this "fire and brimstone" preacher on the role.

"When victims of violence are able to resist the temptation to retaliate, they become the most credible promoters of nonviolent peacemaking."

Pope Francis
Message for World Day of Peace 2017

ARMY FOR PEACE

Suppose that Canada and the United States established large training centers for teaching people nonviolent intervention and formed them into organized units. Suppose the government spent millions of dollars to recruit the finest people into these units, supplying them with salaries and promises of college scholarships, with room and board, and with special lifetime benefits after their period of service. Do you think we'd have a lot of participants? Of course we would.

Suppose the government paid all expenses for these people to go to <location of a current conflict> and practice nonviolent intervention aimed at ending the killing there. The government would provide all the supplies and equipment (far, far less than needed by an armed force) and guarantee benefits to the families of those who were killed or maimed in the line of duty. Everyone left at home would pray for these interveners, hold big rallies and put up yellow ribbons and plaster their cars with bumper stickers for them, and call them all heroes.

"Robert"

    Merciful and loving Creator, we ask you with all our hearts
        to bountifully pour out on our enemies
            whatever will be for their good.
    Above all, give them a sound and uncorrupt mind
        with which they might honor and love you
            and also love us.
    Do not let their hating us turn to their harm.
    Lord, we ask that they be changed, and that we be changed.
    Do not separate them from us by punishing them;
        deal gently with them and join them to us.
    Help us to see that we have all been called to be citizens
        of the everlasting city; let us begin to love each other now
           because love is the end we seek. AMEN

Adapted from a 16th-century English prayer, author unknown

Threatened...

Exploring tough questions facing youth today

1. When someone turns on me or rejects me, my first instinct is to...

2. If I had the power to keep some people from abusing or harming others, I would...

3. There's nothing more important to me in this world than...

4. If someone threatened to destroy [fill in with answer from #3], I would respond by...

>>> "If I could make just one law, it would be that the men who make the decisions to drop bombs would first, every time, have to spend one whole day taking care of a baby. We were not made to do this killing thing, I swear. Back up. It's a big mistake."

Novelist & essayist Barbara Kingsolver, in "God's Wife's Measuring Spoons," *Small Wonders*

God Is a Warrior? : Session 5

Permission is granted to photocopy this handout for use with this session.

Operation Desert Rescue

Adapted from a scenario by David Radcliff

In Real Life
Exploring tough questions facing youth today

Your country is preparing for war against Katestan. The war council has declared war because "our very way of living is at stake." Why? Katestan controls the supply of a crucial mineral used in nearly every high-tech manufacturing process. A few years ago, however, the leadership of Katestan changed, and the new president now plans to "nationalize" the highly profitable mining operation, once controlled by a large corporation in your country. The profits will be turned back over to the Katestani people, who until now have lived in desperate poverty. Katestan is willing to pay the company the market price for its equipment and for the land it owns.

The corporation is understandably angry at this development. They provided many good—although low-paying—jobs for the Katestanis, and they paid to improve the roads and electric service. The president of the company tells his influential government contacts that this is really a national security concern, since anyone who controls the supply of this mineral could use it to blackmail the world. It is too valuable to be left to the control of "some radical third-world leader." Angry and influential stockholders in the company also appeal to their congressional representatives.

To further escalate the crisis, the company recently paid groups of Katestanis to stage violent protests against the takeover of the operation by their government. In response, the Katestan government reacted by killing several dozen people. The company also paid some Katestanis to riot in front of the embassy of your country. This led to fears that the embassy would be overrun and its employees taken captive.

As a result, the war council has put troops in the region on alert. A public relations campaign has begun to prepare the country for war. Images of angry Katestanis are on the television every night. Scenes of riots outside the embassy are shown, although secret cables from the ambassador reassure government leaders that the embassy staff is in no danger. "Special reports" highlight the importance of the mineral that the Katestanis now control and the many jobs that could be lost should access to it be denied. (No one mentions that the Katestanis have never threatened to cut off the supply of the mineral or to raise its price.) Nevertheless, its price on world markets skyrockets as the threat of war looms. News programs feature the backwardness of Katestani life, and note that the majority of Katestanis practice a religion that few people in your country have heard of or understand.

War seems inevitable. The war council vows to "utilize the full range of weapons at our disposal, to restore order to this troubled nation, many of whose citizens have turned to us in their hour of crisis.... Our nation will unleash the power of its armed forces for a decisive end to the reckless course set for Katestan by its illegitimate leadership." The impending war is named "Operation Desert Rescue," over the protests of many members of your government.

1. How can wrong information about the Katestani people and its government be corrected?
2. How can the public be allowed to see Katestanis as real human beings rather than as backwards or "strange" foreigners?
3. What can be done to keep your nation from developing the kinds of weapons that seem to make the war easier because it causes fewer deaths to the soldiers of your country?
4. How can we address the fact that corporations have tremendous influence in our national and international life?
5. How does the problem of the vast differences in wealth between people in different parts of the world contribute to violence? What should we be doing about it?

Permission is granted to photocopy this handout for use with this session.

>>> SESSION 6

LAND FOR SALE >>>

Exploring tough questions facing youth today

>> KEY VERSE

"Yet you, O Lord God, have said to me, 'Buy the field for money and get witnesses'—though the city has been given into the hands of the Chaldeans." (Jeremiah 32:25)

>> FAITH STORY

Jeremiah 32

>> FAITH FOCUS

In 587 B.C.E., the southern kingdom (Judah) was about to fall to the Babylonians. The prophet Jeremiah was under house arrest for predicting the defeat of Judah, which is not what King Zedekiah wanted to hear. While under arrest, Jeremiah's cousin offered to sell him a piece of family property. Jeremiah made the purchase, even though the city was about to be overrun by the enemy and the people taken into captivity. Some might say this was an unwise investment. The Lord, however, had told Jeremiah that, "Houses and fields and vineyards shall again be bought in this land" (v. 15). Thus, it was an investment in the future, showing confidence that the exiles would return.

>> SESSION GOAL

Encourage participants to live fully in the world, acting on its behalf, in spite of the often-discouraging threat of violence.

>> Materials needed and advance preparation

- Recruit a "visiting prophet" (see Focus)
- Chalkboard/chalk or newsprint/markers
- Two copies of the handout sheet for Session 6, and two readers
- Bibles
- Writing paper and pencils/pens

TEACHING PLAN

1. FOCUS 5 minutes

Invite a person to visit as a modern-day prophet. The person should look and act the part of someone concerned with the "way things are heading" in the congregation, the larger Church, in the community-at-large or in the nation. The prophet tells the group in no uncertain terms that unless things change for the better, things will quickly change for the worse. What is God expecting of these people in this time? How have we failed to live up to this? Have the prophet end the five-minute tirade with one of the following scriptures that links future judgment or prosperity with present morality or faithfulness (cf. Micah 2:1-4; Amos 4:1-3), then depart.

Then ask, *What purpose does a prophet serve? Who would you consider a modern-day prophet? Does our society pay much attention to those who call loudly for change and renewal? Does the church pay attention to such people, even when the people are calling the Church to change and renewal?*

In Real Life | God Is a Warrior?   45

"If someday they take the radio station from us, if they close down the newspaper, if they don't let us speak, if they kill all the priests and the bishop, too, and you are left a people without priests, each one of you must become God's microphone, each one of you must become a messenger, a prophet."

St. Oscar Romero

2. CONNECT 5 minutes

Ask the group to list five to seven of the most troubling aspects of our world today. (Examples include: racial conflict, water and food security, child abuse, climate change, economic inequality, etc.) Go down the list, asking whether the group has hope that each of these has a possibility of being resolved in their lifetime. Rate each item on the list (1 = little hope, to 4 = very confident) to signify the level of optimism that the problem will be resolved in their lifetime. Add the total, then divide by the number of people in the group to give each problem a "Hope Quotient." If there is not much optimism of resolution, ask what our response should be. Should we give up and give in? Should we keep trying to make the world better?

3. EXPLORE THE BIBLE 10 minutes

Shift to this activity by saying: *Sometimes it's hard to have hope for the future. But the only way to have a future is to maintain hope. Here's how the prophet Jeremiah did it....*

Have two members of the group reenact the story of Jeremiah purchasing a parcel of property from his relative just as the city is ready to fall (on handout sheet).

After the skit, reinforce the plot of the story by reading Jeremiah 32:1-15.

4. APPLY 20 minutes

Have participants write their own prophecy of the future. Ask them to take into consideration factors that might concern a present-day prophet—the health of the environment, the growing gap between the rich and poor, the development of increasingly sophisticated military weaponry, child abuse, substance abuse, food security, etc. In a similar manner, the ancient prophets looked at the condition of the world, and particularly at God's people, and then told what would happen based on the people's level of faithfulness or unfaithfulness. The future was an outcome of the present.

Give the group this outline for their prophecy (see Jer. 7:1-15):

    a. Get the attention of the audience (the "Hear the word of the Lord!" section)
    b. The change that's needed in the lives of the people (the "Change your ways" section)
    c. What will happen if the needed changes are made (the "If you act justly" section)
    d. What will happen if the old behavior continues (the "I will cast you out of my sight" section)

Have the participants share their oracles. Some may want to create symbolic actions to accompany their prophecies (an example of symbolic action taken by Jeremiah is his wearing a yoke around his neck to symbolize Israel's submission to the Babylonians—chapter 27, vv. 1-2).

5. RESPOND 5 minutes

》》 Option A: What would be symbolic actions the group could take to show their hope for the world in spite of its problems? Use some of the problems listed above. For instance, in spite of serious environmental problems, the group could conduct a roadside clean-up project. Don't forget a portable sign telling passersby who you are, what you're doing, and why you're doing it. And what about local newspaper coverage?

End your planning session with prayer, asking God to give you the words and energy to spread the word of hope, and to act on it.

»» Option B: Practice Gratitude

End your session giving each person an opportunity to name one thing they are grateful for at this moment. Practicing gratitude pokes holes in dark coverings of despair, and allows us to imagine solutions. Another way is to pause periodically in your day and notice something good within your sight or hearing, and say "yes" to it: "yes" to that spreading tree, "yes" to that flying ball, "yes" to the warm blanket, "yes" to the raspberry. As you do this, notice what happens inside you.

INSIGHTS FROM SCRIPTURE

The sixth century B.C.E. (Before Common Era) was a period of extreme anxiety and forced relocation for the people of the southern kingdom of Judah. Their world was coming apart at the seams—the Babylonians were about to march them off into exile—and away from the land promised them by God. More than a political calamity, this was a crisis of faith. How could their faith in God carry them through this time of disruption, when God's very presence and promise must have seemed distressingly remote?

The role of Jeremiah the prophet is a fascinating one. On the one hand, he was clearly a prophet of doom, telling the nation in no uncertain terms that unless it changed its ways, it could not and would not survive. While citizens wanted to believe that God would never allow such a fate to befall the "chosen" people, Jeremiah's prophecies were a clear and present reminder that this would indeed happen—and that their defeat would be allowed by God!

On the other hand, one of the most hopeful deeds in the Bible is Jeremiah's purchase of the field at Anathoth. Here at this critical moment—the nation in its death throes, the Babylonian army on the verge of victory—Jeremiah's purchase was a poignant reminder that though God's people were to be driven away, they would return.

»» CHOOSE–CYNICISM, OR RETURN TO LIFE

This story certainly held power for the people of Israel at this decisive moment in their history. It holds power for us as well. There *are* reasons to be cynical about prospects for our own future. From climate change, to the growing gap between rich and poor, to genocide, to food insecurity, to family break-ups, to street violence—today's people of faith, including youth, have many reasons to despair. And these impending or present catastrophes should not be downplayed! Any prophet worth a dash of salt would have harsh words for our way of living and its consequences.

But a prophet would likewise look for ways to reassure God's people that in spite of the dire situation, there can be a brighter day ahead, should we return to God's ways. In what ways can we—the faith community, the youth of the faith community—hold together both the warnings of coming difficulties and the assurance of God's ongoing care? What are concrete signs we can provide for ourselves and our world?

"When discouraged and despairing, remember this: The great cathedrals of the Middle Ages took 200-300 years to build. Most workers in those cathedrals never saw the whole building, never prayed there. We who are building the cathedral of peace, maybe we won't see it either. We will die before it is completed, and yet we are going to build it."

Dorothee Sölle and C.F. Beyers Naudé, *Hope for Faith*

"I get to choose whether to hang it up or hang on, and I hang on because I was born to do it, like everyone else. I insist that I can do something right, if I try. I insist that you can, too, that in fact you already are, and there's a whole lot more where this came from.... [I] conquer my own despair by doing what little I can.... The possibility of a kinder future, the existence of God—these are just two of many things that fall into the category I would label 'impossible to prove, and proof is not the point.' Faith has a life of its own."

Barbara Kingsolver, "God's Wife's Measuring Spoons," *Small Wonders*

"Nada te turbe, nada te espante. Quien a Dios tiene nada le falta. Nada te turbe, nada te espante. Sólo Dios basta."

(Translation: Let nothing trouble you, let nothing frighten you. Whoever has God lacks nothing. God alone is enough.)

St. Teresa of Ávila, 1515-1582

"I believe the gospels are the best story we have. They are the singular counter-narrative to our consumerist, war-mongering, media-saturated, technologized, dehumanized, death-oriented culture. The story of the gospels... cannot be proven; and we cannot accept the story on faith alone; but we love the story so much that we want it to be true. To will the story into existence by our own living testimony to its veracity, thus giving witness to our deepest hopes for humanity - that is what attracted me as a young person to the Catholic Worker, and that is what attracts young people to this day."

Jeff Dietrich, *Broken and Shared: Food, Dignity, and the Poor on Los Angeles' Skid Row*.

Buy a Little Hope
(a skit from Jeremiah 32)

In Real Life — Exploring tough questions facing youth today

Scene opens with Jeremiah under house arrest. The official reason is suspicion of desertion; in reality, Jeremiah is indicted for his prophecy, which predicted the fall of Jerusalem in 587 B.C.E. (Before Common Era). Other prophets predicted the success of the Israelites; thus, they were more popular with political leaders.

Voice offstage: Jeremiah, your cousin is going to come to you and offer to let you buy his field in Anathoth: As next of kin, you have the right to purchase it.

Jeremiah: Ah,.... God, if you'd excuse me, your Godship, er, you see, this country is about to be overrun by the Babylonians and everyone is going to be shipped off into slavery. Some people might not think that this was the best time to be investing in real estate....

Voice: Well, I'm not "some people"!! Did you ever think I might know some things you don't know, Jeremiah? You must buy this land to show the people that someday I will bring you back to this place. Besides, who knows, that little plot of your cousin's might make a nice site for a community garden some day!

Jeremiah: *(with sarcasm)* Oh, I get it. I buy this land from my cousin, my cousin gets my money, which may come in handy if we're going on a long road trip. I get a piece of land right here in beautiful Babylonia-occupied Jerusalem, while all of us are taken off to a place hundreds of miles away, probably never to return. Is that it?

Voice: You forgot about the community garden.

Jeremiah: Yeah, I'm marching off to Babylonia for seeds!

Voice: Have I ever led you wrong, Jeremiah?

Jeremiah: Well, there was the time I prayed for the answers on my Hebrew history exam…

Voice: As little as you studied, you didn't have a prayer! Get serious, Jeremiah. I need someone to show these people that they can have hope, even in a desperate situation. They need to believe that someday they will return to this land. You're the one who can make them believe. But first of all, *you've* got to believe. You do believe what I'm telling you, don't you, Jeremiah?

Jeremiah: *(slight pause)* Yes, God, I believe. You really think a community garden would thrive in that location?...

God Is a Warrior? : Session 6

Permission is granted to photocopy this handout for use with this session.

>>> EXTENDER SESSION
(best used after Session 5)

>> Option A: Gandhi

>> SESSION GOAL
Give participants a concrete example of the success of nonviolent action for change.

Plan: Watch *Gandhi* at someone's home or at an evening session in the youth room (it's about three hours long, so you may choose to only watch parts). This film portrays the nonviolent struggle of the people of India against the British colonial rulers. There is some violence portrayed, however, on the part of colonial rulers. Follow the film with a discussion about how well you believe nonviolent action worked in the emergence of the nation of India.

>> Option B: Dead Man Walking

>> SESSION GOAL
Give participants a concrete example of the success of nonviolent action for change.

Plan: View and discuss the film *Dead Man Walking* (some graphic language, reenactment of a rape scene). It is the story of Sister Helen Prejean's journey through the system of capital punishment. She confronts both the plight of the condemned and the rage of the bereaved. The film is "a journey into the issue that will bring people to places in their hearts they hadn't been before," Prejean says.

What drives her witness, Prejean explains, is a desire "to articulate what I personally believe about Jesus and the ethical thrust he gave to humankind: an impetus toward compassion, a preference for disarming enemies without humiliating and destroying them, and a solidarity with poor and suffering people." Prejean insists that the church's place is on both sides of the death penalty debate, with the families of victims and with the convicted killers.

Here is an online discussion guide for *Dead Man Walking*:
www.spiritualityandpractice.com/films/vvcfeatures.php?id=15404

>> Materials needed and advance preparation

- Media player
- View the movie *Gandhi* (Option A)
- View the movie *Dead Man Walking* (Option B)

"Why are deadly weapons being sold to those who plan to inflict untold suffering on individuals and society? Sadly, the answer, we know, is simply for money: money that is drenched in blood, often innocent blood. In the face of this shameful and culpable silence, it is our duty to confront the problem and stop the arms trade."

Pope Francis
Address to U.S. Congress,
September 24, 2015

Option C: Is War Ever Just?

(adapted from *Decide for Peace,* by Eddy Hall)

SESSION GOAL

Help participants measure the ethical value of recent wars using the just war theory.

Plan: For the first 300 years of Christianity, early church leaders taught pacifism. As soon as Constantine began forming a church-state alliance, participation in the Roman army came to be considered normal, and the theologian Augustine developed a teaching—called the "just war" theory—to explain how a person could be both a good Christian and a good soldier. Augustine taught that war, if waged according to strict guidelines, could be consistent with the law of love. "Love," he wrote, "does not exclude wars of mercy waged by the good."[1]

The rules of the just war view are as follows:

1. **Just cause.** Only defensive war is legitimate.
2. **Just intention.** The goal of the war must be to secure a just peace for all involved. Revenge, conquest, and economic gain are not acceptable reasons for fighting.
3. **Last resort.** War can be fought only when all negotiations and compromises have been tried and failed.
4. **Formal declaration.** Since only governments have the moral right to use military force, the highest government authorities must formally declare war.
5. **Limited objectives.** Since the purpose must be peace, objectives such as unconditional surrender or the destruction of a nation's economic or political institutions are never appropriate.
6. **Proportionate means.** The weapons and force used should be no greater than needed to achieve a just peace. Total annihilation is not an option.
7. **Noncombatant immunity.** People not actively contributing to the conflict—including civilians, casualties, and prisoners of war—should be immune from attack.[2]

Bible study: Most wars are fought for selfish reasons. But are there ever times when people might fight for unselfish reasons? The New Testament suggests a couple of possibilities.

1. In John 18:36, what did Jesus say would be an unselfish reason for his followers to fight? Even though that would have been unselfish, why did Jesus say fighting was inappropriate?

The holy wars of Israel can be seen as wars on behalf of God, since God's realm at that time was identified with the political nation of Israel. Since in our age God's reign is not identified with any nation—it is "not from this world"—Jesus forbids fighting on behalf of that kingdom. If the Christians of the Middle Ages had understood the radical Jesus Way, the Crusades might never have happened.

2. What was Peter's motive in trying to kill Malchus in Matthew 26:51 and John 18:10? Was he unselfish? What does Jesus' response tell us about this motive (Mt. 26:52-54)?

The desire to protect another person, especially an innocent victim, is a noble motive. Jesus' rebuke names three problems with Peter's use of violence to defend Jesus:

a. violence leads to more violence;

b. violence is not needed because God can deliver miraculously; and

c. in this case Jesus needed to lay down his life to fulfill God's purpose for him.

Peter's motive was right; his method was wrong. What guidance, if any, do you feel you could draw from these words of Jesus if you were considering killing to protect innocent people?

Discuss:

1. Think of the war in which your country fought that you know the most about, either a recent war or a historical war you've studied. Measure it against the standards of a "just war."

    a. Was the cause just? Was it a purely defensive war? What was being defended?

    b. Was your country's only goal to secure a fair peace for all involved? Were there no selfish motives?

    c. Was war a last resort? Were all nonviolent alternatives tried before resorting to war?

    d. Did the highest government authorities formally declare war?

    e. Were the objectives of the war strictly limited? Was care taken not to destroy the political or economic institutions of the enemy? Was there no demand for unconditional surrender?

    f. Was the force used no greater than what was needed to win a just peace?

    g. Did your country take great care to ensure that your enemy's civilians, prisoners of war, and casualties were not exposed to attack?

2. Can you think of any wars that have been carried out *within* the just war rules? If so, which ones?

3. If your country were to follow strictly the rules for a just war, what practical differences would that make? Which of the principles would be most difficult to implement?

4. Do you think it's a good idea for Christians to try to hold their governments accountable to just war standards? Why or why not?

5. One of the rules of "just war" is that all nonviolent alternatives to resolving the conflict must be tried before resorting to war. Faith-based pacifists believe there are always nonviolent alternatives to war, though the remaining nonviolent alternatives may involve great suffering and even the deaths of those seeking to make peace. The martyrdom of peacemakers can be a most powerful force for peace.

> In 2016, a Vatican conference co-hosted by the Pontifical Council for Justice and Peace and the Pax Christi International argued that just war theory should be rejected, saying it is out-of-date, has been used to justify violent conflicts too often, and that non-violent approaches should always be pursued.

Do you agree that there are always alternatives to war so long as the peacemakers are prepared to consider creative options and pay any personal price?

Most Christians have probably never seriously considered trying to apply Jesus' teachings to this issue, and so their views are shaped more by their political surroundings than by their faith, and they approve of almost every war their country fights. Some of these would say they believe in the just war view, but they don't really know what the just war view is. What they mean is "I support any war I think is for a just cause." As we have seen, that is only one of several criteria a war must meet to qualify theologically as a "just war." Christians who take seriously just war principles will apply those standards to *each* war to determine which wars are worthy of their support.

A Christian pacifist is a conscientious objector to participating in all wars. By contrast, a Christian who subscribes to the just war view is a *selective* conscientious objector, objecting to participation in all wars that fail to measure up to the just war standards. Since few, if any, modern wars measure up to all the just war standards, a Christian who takes seriously the just war view may end up being a pacifist in practice even if not in theory, and may go a lifetime without finding a single war worthy of support under those guidelines. This is especially likely to be true in light of what Ronald Sider points out about war being used only as a last resort. Since we live in a time when a wide variety of nonviolent alternatives have been demonstrated to be more effective than war—that is, they achieve their goal with less injury and loss of life—it may be impossible ever to say that the nonviolent alternatives have been exhausted.

1. Quoted in Roland H. Bainton, *Christian Attitudes Toward War and Peace*
2. Arthur F. Holmes, "The Just War" in *War: Four Christian Views*, ed. Robert G. Clouse

Exploring tough questions facing youth today

CLUELESS AND CALLED
Discipleship and the Gospel of Mark

What does it take to be a disciple? This study of the Gospel of Mark focuses on the requirements for following Jesus' way and the abundant life that is ours as a result. (5 sessions)

DO MIRACLES HAPPEN?
Signs and Wonders in the Gospel of John

The greatest miracle, recorded in John 1:14 and 3:16, is the miracle of God's love that became flesh and lived among us. But John also included examples of what we more traditionally think of as miracles: the wonder of abundance from little; healing; signs of impossibility and faith; and the resurrection. (5 sessions)

DO THE RIGHT THING
Ethics Shaped by Faith

How do you know what's right and what's wrong? Even when you figure it out, the right thing is often the unpopular or unpleasant choice. This unit offers participants a clearer sense of what it means to claim a faith identity, a foundation that can help them sort out the gritty details of ethics shaped by faith. (6 sessions)

FIGHT RIGHT
A Christian Approach to Conflict Resolution

This unit will help youth understand conflict and its function. They will learn how they can be honest and loving, and explore how conflict can be used for positive results. They will also learn ways to enhance their communication skills. 1 Corinthians. (5 sessions)

GOD IS A WARRIOR?
Violence in the Bible

The Bible challenges us to be reconciled to one another and work for justice. So what do we do with the stories that seem to condone violence or even encourage it? A discussion of issues in the Old and New Testaments. (6 sessions)

HOW DO YOU KNOW?
Wisdom in the Bible

Wisdom literature teaches us that we gain knowledge of the world, ourselves, and God through experience and observation. This unit provides practical, hands-on wisdom to help young people avoid life's snares and grow closer to God. Proverbs, Job, Ecclesiastes. (5 sessions)

HOW TO BE A TRUE FRIEND
The Bible Reveals Friendship's Heart

To be a friend takes skill. Help youth discover the secrets of friendship through various stories from the Old and New Testament. (6 sessions)

HOW TO READ THE BIBLE
Building Skills for Bible Study

What kind of book is the Bible? What does this book mean to me? This unit looks at the Bible as revelation, as history, as literature. Selected scripture. (5 sessions)

KEEPING THE GARDEN
A Faith Response to God's Creation

If Christians believe that God made the world, we do not need any more compelling reason to care for it than that God has handed us a treasure to hold and protect. This unit gets beyond trendy environmentalism and challenges youth to see environmental awareness as a religious issue. Genesis. (6 sessions)

MANTRAS, MENORAHS, AND MINARETS
Encountering Other Faiths

How is Christianity different from other faiths? Why do others believe the way they do? This study can give youth a new appreciation for the uniqueness of Jesus. Selected scripture. (5 sessions)

SALT, LIGHT, AND THE GOOD LIFE
The Beatitudes and the Sermon on the Mount

What can youth expect in a life of discipleship? This unit explores the Sermon on the Mount under four main sections: the Beatitudes, Salt and Light, Jesus and the Law, and Heavenly Teachings. Matthew 5. (6 sessions)

A SPECK IN THE UNIVERSE
The Bible on Self-Esteem and Peer Pressure

Discover God's unconditional love and acceptance of all people. This study will show positive ways to have one's life make a difference, and help youth find ways to resist negative peer pressure and turn it into positive action. (6 sessions)

THE RADICAL REIGN
Parables of Jesus

Jesus used parables to reveal what the kingdom of God is like, and how God relates to us. This study highlights how the parables reveal God's reign as radically different from the world we live in, and what that means for the Christian life. (6 sessions)

TESTING THE WATERS
Basic Tenets of Faith

Discover the biblical roots for the central Christian concepts of covenant, community, and baptism. This short course is a way to test the (baptismal) waters of Christianity before diving in, or review the basics for those who already have. (6 sessions)

WHO IS GOD?
Engaging the Mystery

God is beyond human comprehension, yet desires to be known. These sessions focus on the way we get clues about and glimpses of God from the Bible, God's creation, and church tradition. Selected scripture. (5 sessions)

www.ingramcontent.com/pod-product-compliance
Lightning Source LLC
Chambersburg PA
CBHW080408170426
43193CB00016B/2849